Wilfred Owen's
Shrewsbury

Fish-street, Shrewsbury.

Evacustes A. Phipson, 1906

WILFRED OWEN'S SHREWSBURY

from the Severn to Poetry and War

HELEN MCPHAIL

LOGASTON PRESS

First published in 2018 by Logaston Press
The Holme, Church Road, Eardisley HR3 6NJ
www.logastonpress.co.uk
An imprint of Fircone Books Ltd.

ISBN 978-1-910839-25-6

Text copyright © Helen McPhail, 2018
Illustrations copyright © Shropshire Archives and Bodleian Library unless otherwise acknowledged
in Image Credits on p. 129.

Designed and typeset by Richard Wheeler.
Cover design by Richard Wheeler (based on a sketch by John Dangerfield).

Printed and bound in Poland.

British Library Catalogue in Publishing Data.
A CIP catalogue record for this book is available from the British Library.

CONTENTS

Acknowledgements   vii

Maps   viii

INTRODUCTION   1

1 THE PEOPLE, THE PLACE   5

2 SCHOOL DAYS   29

3 SPREADING HORIZONS   51

4 TRANSITIONS   75

5 DESTINATIONS   99

AFTERMATH   121

Appendix 1: Family Tree   126

Appendix 2: Roundel Poem   127

Select Bibliography   128

Image Credits   129

Index   131

Acknowledgements

I HAVE drawn on many different kinds of record, published and personal, and am deeply grateful for the time, conversations and encouragement I have had in Shrewsbury and elsewhere. Very many people have helped with this book and I would particularly like to thank Gordon Dickins and Andrew Pattison for their time, knowledge and experience, Tony Carr for historical checking and Ian Musty for the history of the United Reformed Church. Mary McKenzie and the staff of Shropshire Archives have been consistently supportive and helpful, and I am extremely grateful for their guidance. Peter and Elizabeth Owen have been patient and generous with information and advice over many years, and have shown great tolerance in sharing their knowledge. Richard and Su Wheeler of Logaston Press have been steadily thoughtful and helpful in preparing this book, and any errors that appear here are entirely mine.

Jacky Duminy as Mayor of Ors has been a wonderful source of support and interest in France, and has contributed greatly to francophone recognition of Wilfred Owen. Thanks go too to John Dangerfield for the cover design and preparation of maps for this book, and to Liz Kessler for her photograph of 'Symmetry' at the time of its installation in the grounds of Shrewsbury Abbey in 1993, the centenary of Wilfred Owen's birth. All of those involved at that time remember Robert Hutchison for his warmth and immense knowledge, enthusiasm and hard work as the first Chairman of the Wilfred Owen Association in establishing the modern memory of the poet in Shrewsbury.

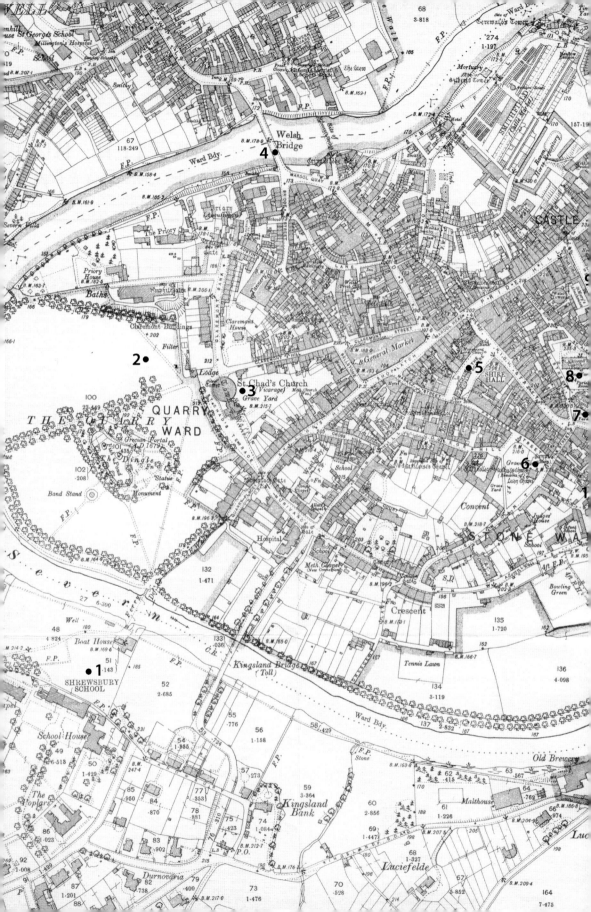

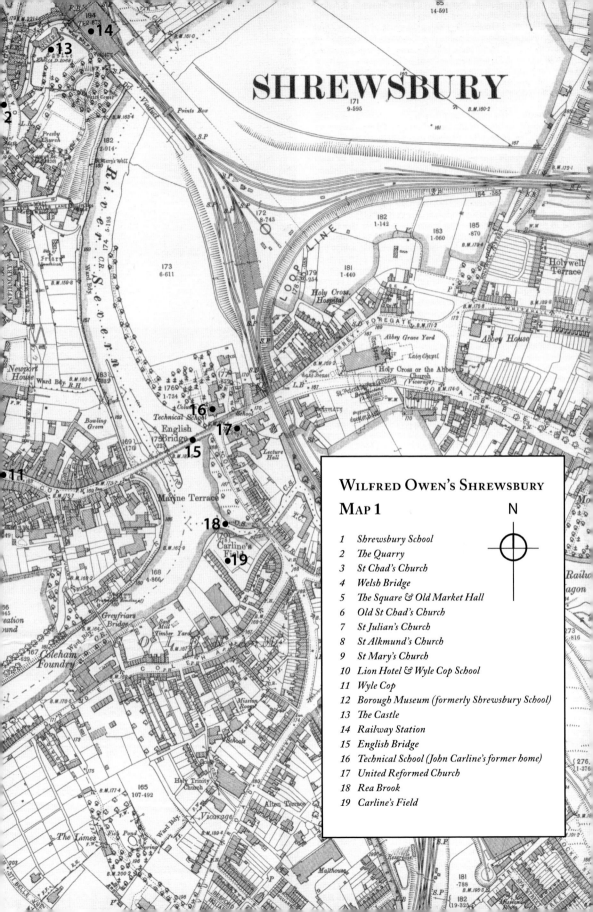

SHREWSBURY

WILFRED OWEN'S SHREWSBURY

MAP 1   N

1   Shrewsbury School
2   The Quarry
3   St Chad's Church
4   Welsh Bridge
5   The Square & Old Market Hall
6   Old St Chad's Church
7   St Julian's Church
8   St Alkmund's Church
9   St Mary's Church
10 Lion Hotel & Wyle Cop School
11 Wyle Cop
12 Borough Museum (formerly Shrewsbury School)
13 The Castle
14 Railway Station
15 English Bridge
16 Technical School (John Carline's former home)
17 United Reformed Church
18 Rea Brook
19 Carline's Field

WILFRED OWEN'S SHREWSBURY

MAP 2

N

20 Cherry Orchard
21 Hawthorn Villas
22 Future site of 'Mahim'
23 Ferry
24 Racecourse & Grandstand
25 Cleveland Place
26 Underdale Road
27 Monkmoor Street
28 Railway 'set-down' halt
29 Holywell Terrace
30 Horse Fair
31 The Abbey
32 Shropshire & Montgomeryshire
    Light Railway
33 Midland Railway Carriage
    & Wagon Works (subsequently
    prisoner-of-war camp 1914–19)
34 Abbey Foregate
35 Lord Hill's Column

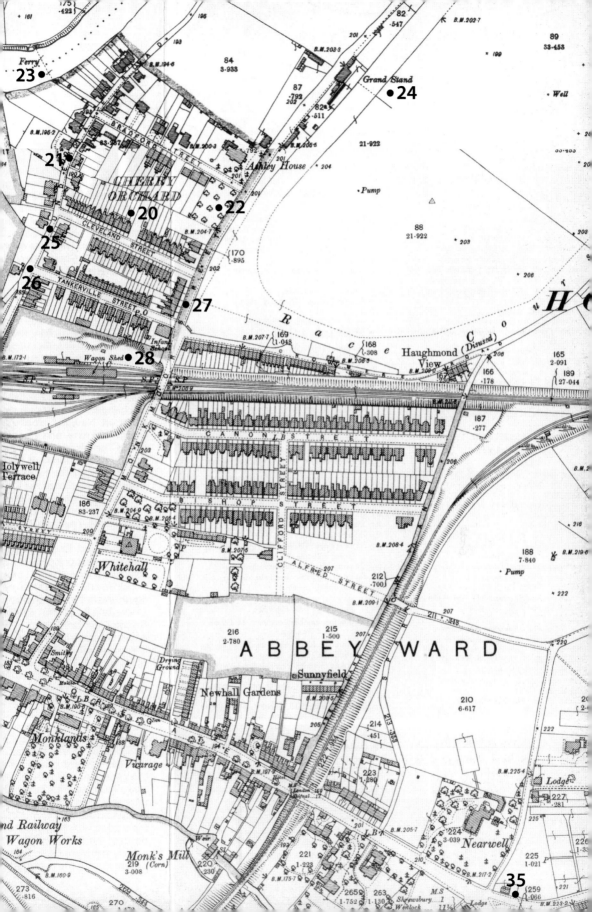

INTRODUCTION

B OTH Shrewsbury town and Wilfred Owen attract considerable interest. Visitors come to explore the town, appreciate its style and discover its landscape, picturesque setting and historic past; and in the century since his death Wilfred Owen has become increasingly well-known to the general public and specialists as one of the most significant voices of the First World War.

This book is not a comprehensive social history of a rural county town in the early twentieth century; nor is it a literary guide or anthology of Wilfred Owen's poems. It is about a future poet's formative years growing up in this place at this time. The locations, atmosphere and events in pre-1914 Shrewsbury contribute much to our understanding of the background details of everyday life for the Owen family, and of the surroundings in which Wilfred Owen spent his teenage years. Elements of his early childhood in Birkenhead, and later in Dunsden, Bordeaux and during the First World War also provide settings and events crucial to his adult imagination and creativity.

As an approach, this inevitably leaves out much material about the centre and the suburbs of Shrewsbury which has been published in detail elsewhere. Rather, this approach is intended to give something of the flavour of life for one individual and his family at a specific time, before the events and profound consequences of the First World War. Beyond this, Wilfred Owen has been the subject of full-length biographies, literary studies and anthologies, which provide extensive details and show his place in English twentieth-century literature.

Bringing together surviving material about the town and this particular household in order to examine the poet's schoolboy years is fascinating and frequently frustrating. Thanks to his mother, Susan, we have Wilfred's letters from a very early age, with a lively narrative of incidents and activities, or thoughtful reflections on his life, hopes and anxieties. In addition we have his brother Harold's memoirs (*Journey from Obscurity*), written when he was in his sixties. Here he recounts his own varied and adventurous life, but with particular awareness of Wilfred's creative life and literary

Fig. 1 **(left)** *Wilfred Owen in a sailor suit (c.1895). The boat was made for him by his father.*

Fig. 2 *Tom, Susan and Wilfred at Plas Wilmot in 1891. Susan is in mourning for her mother.*

Fig. 3 *Wilfred (rear) with Harold, Mary and Colin on a swing (c.1902).*

Fig. 4 *Colin, Mary, Harold, Wilfred and Susan (c.1902). Apparently taken at the same time as Fig. 3.*

significance in his description of the whole family and their relationships. Harold, too, writes vividly, although he never ventures into poetry. Inevitably, writing so many decades after the earliest events in his life, there are occasional inaccuracies of date, or of details of the presence or absence of a family member.

Despite Wilfred's close relationship with his mother, he grew to understand that he must protect her from his mature patterns of thought, and experiences of life away from home and family life. Similarly, Harold in later life was almost obsessively careful to avoid any possible offence or indiscretion in making Wilfred's letters and his own memoirs available for publication. With both brothers we are frequently obliged to consider what is written, or what is presented for publication, in the light of modern knowledge and attitudes. It becomes clear that many subjects could not easily be broached with their parents, in the eternal gulf between parental beliefs and experience, and the ideas, talents and ambitions developing in their children. Between them, however, these two very different brothers have provided a strong picture of themselves, their times and the circumstances of their lives.

The family's surroundings in the years before 1914 can be explored through archived photographs, with an observant eye for street patterns and the demands of modern traffic. The many surviving buildings help to recreate the past for the visitor on foot, but the townscape as a whole repays examination and an understanding of how it developed over the decades.

It may be a statement of the obvious but, from the point of view of both residents and visitors, the most significant feature in Shrewsbury is the River Severn. The railway system comes a close second in forming the pattern of streets, houses and traffic; but any account of life in the town, particularly in the early twentieth century, must recognise the importance of the river and its influence over the centuries. It shaped the town, and much later the railways both influenced the street pattern and encouraged the town's expansion.

Shrewsbury was established on this site, probably in the ninth century, in order to take advantage of the defensive position inside the river loop, with the shallows to be controlled and allow access. After the Norman Conquest, the hilly ground inside the river bends made the narrow neck of the loop a dominant site for a substantial castle.

This long river, winding down from the mountains of Mid-Wales towards the Atlantic, has shaped the town and more or less everything in it. Its floods, frequent and not always predictable, have ensured the survival of open space along its banks (notably now the Quarry park), and of the open fields up and down stream, where the risk of flooding made building unwise, or simply impossible. Flood defences – natural and man-made – have tamed the river to some extent; however, the expanding town required workshops, quays and houses near the English and Welsh bridges in order to support river trade as well as accommodation outside the cramped town centre.

The Industrial Revolution made full use of the river in manufacturing and for transport, and turned Shrewsbury into an early centre of fresh thinking, inventiveness and engineering. The growing railway system recognised its value as a practical junction, with tracks spreading out towards established and growing industrial areas in the Ironbridge Gorge, the Midlands, Manchester and North Wales, and the coalfields and iron-works of South Wales.

Today's Shrewsbury is a fine blend of many centuries of building, rebuilding, redesigning, transport and patterns of residential life. The twisting street lay-out and the consequence of the tightly restricting River Severn are still confusing for drivers in the town centre, with the many linking 'shuts' or passageways providing pedestrian access in all directions. Many old buildings have gone, but many still survive, for Shrewsbury was spared excessive Victorian redevelopment. Ancient half-timber construction may lurk behind later brick façades, and the eighteenth and nineteenth centuries are widely identifiable in their many different styles.

The river itself emerges consistently as a defining baseline for where to live and how to move around. Throughout the town's history it has been one of its most important features, initially protective and later as a contributing feature in local industry, activity and leisure. It is quite easy for the visitor to overlook areas outside the river loop, but we are fortunate that in Cherry Orchard (the residential area where the Owens lived in Shrewsbury) both family houses can be identified. This distinctive area provides a good background to Wilfred's family life as he grew to adulthood in Shrewsbury, and to his grounding for the unknown future.

The steady growth of Wilfred Owen's reputation since his death in the closing days of the First World War, aged only 25, can be set alongside our understanding of that war and its world-wide effects. His poetry has contributed greatly to changes in our response to historic events, the literature around warfare, and attitudes among both combatants and civilians. From the family home to Shrewsbury Abbey, the site of the old Technical School beside the river, the old museum and the busy railway station stretching across the River Severn, we can follow the pattern of everyday life and recognise some missed opportunities or might-have-beens; and despite changes, we can imagine the town in the 1900s and its features that would have been so familiar as to become almost invisible.

What has been particularly striking at this centenary moment is the range of names that have faded, and the work of others who have emerged to become increasingly well-known and influential. Wilfred Owen is now one of the most frequently quoted writers; one who has provided reassurance, warning and strength to innumerable readers, in his own remarkable English or in translation into many languages. Uniquely, he is also acclaimed in France, the country that he loved and where he is buried in a British military cemetery.

1   THE PEOPLE, THE PLACE
our better prospects in Shrewsbury

O N 11 November 1918 the church bells rang out for Armistice Day, and Tom and Susan Owen could reasonably begin to feel that a more hopeful future might finally be possible. All three of their sons were away serving the nation: Colin in England in the recently-created Royal Air Force, Harold far out at sea in the Royal Naval Reserve – and Wilfred in the army, on active service in France. In one of those bitter ironies that sticks in the mind, it was on this of all days that the fateful telegram was delivered to their door with its bald announcement: Wilfred had been killed in action on 4 November, exactly a week earlier.

More than a decade earlier, when the young Owen family took the train with all their possessions from Birkenhead to Shrewsbury in January 1907, several things were clear. Tom had a good position ahead of him in a familiar place and a steady future in the British railway system. Susan missed Oswestry, her sisters and her sheltered childhood; Birkenhead was not an easy place in which to live with a young family if money was tight. Harold was strong and well-grown but a difficult child when it came to education. Mary was quiet, very small and young for her age, and Colin was loved and petted and cared for by the whole family.

As for Wilfred, the eldest child and Susan's special concern, two things stood out in his thirteen-year-old mind: that he was leaving his school life at Birkenhead Institute, which had been friendly, happy and successful – and that he was going to be a poet. On a spring holiday at the age of ten, alone with his mother at Broxton in the wooded hills of north Cheshire, he had plunged wholeheartedly into the quiet beauties of an idyllic rural setting. His mind expanded and found expression. His early education and reading of the Victorian poets had filled his mind with dreams, and the language in which to define them. The landscape seized him with an enduring poetic vision based on ancient legends, history, Christianity, romantic story-telling and brave adventures in a heroic past.

Tom and Susan Owen and their four children arrived in Shrewsbury on a cold, wet night, and it is unlikely that they noticed much as they rattled through the town in their cab from the station. Down Wyle Cop, over the English Bridge, past the Technical School on the left, under the railway viaduct and past the Abbey, bear left round to Underdale Road to find Tom's parents waiting for them in Hawthorn Villas. The young family spent their first few days here – it probably felt cramped, but it was a good base while they looked for their own accommodation. Apart from the inevitable bustle and anxieties around a family with young children travelling with their luggage and packages, the Owen family probably aroused little casual attention on their arrival. However, as Harold's memoirs and Wilfred's letters show, there were many qualities of character and attitude that expressed each separate identity and this move from Birkenhead meant different things to each of them.

Tom was to be Assistant Superintendent at Shrewsbury Station, a significant post at one of the town's most important institutions. It was a fine prospect given his modest start in life, with corresponding advances in both status and income. Arriving to take up a central administrative post at the centre of the town's impressive railway station, he was a vigorous and sturdy man, not particularly tall, upright and well turned-out, with a quickness of thought and action which often clashed with his wife's quieter and more thoughtful instincts. In family life, as Harold described later in his memoirs, Tom could be quick to argue or assert and found his adolescent children hard to direct, but he was devoted to their prospects and welfare. He particularly enjoyed their company out of doors and worried about their future.

Born in 1862 and brought up in Nantwich, Tom left school at 15 to earn his own way in the world, with a strong sense of independence and his parents' plain, hardworking life. His father was a tailor, and his mother a waistcoat maker who later turned her hand to running a grocery and clothes shop. Tom's first job, as a clerk at Oswestry station, was followed in 1880 by the one real adventure of his life: working his way out to India by sea, he spent four years with the Great Indian and Peninsula Railways. Very little is known about this period of his life, but on his return he joined the Great Western and London & North Western Joint Railways at Shrewsbury station. Still a bachelor, he lodged here with his parents (his father was by now a manager for Maddox & Company, for many years one of Shrewsbury's leading clothes shops).

As a railway employee Tom could use cheap railway travel to maintain his sporting and social friendships formed earlier in Oswestry, not least with the Shaw family there. Later, after his marriage to Susan Shaw, he became stationmaster at Woodside, the terminus station of the Joint Railways Line in Birkenhead, at the height of the city's expansion. He would miss the energy and drive, the bustle and the sense of the whole world coming and going along the River Mersey and its docks; but his earlier years in Shrewsbury had introduced him to a range of sociable pleasures. As a young man he

Fig. 5 *Birkenhead Institute, where Wilfred enjoyed his primary education (c.1890).*

had enjoyed cricket and football, singing (he had a fine voice) and the meetings of the Abbey Foregate Literary Society for talks from writers and travellers.

This later move to Shrewsbury in 1907 represented promotion for Tom in a busy station with six railway lines radiating out from it, and where he had reasonable (but ultimately disappointed) hopes of further promotion. The railways contributed substantially to the local economy, providing employment and requiring plenty of modest housing for the staff at all levels. The scale of the system can best be seen on a map of the town and suburbs, showing the amount of space occupied by platforms, embankments, tracks and freight yards. The town expanded around the station and goods yards, and the multiple tracks and bridges resembled the river in their effect on the street pattern and growing suburbs. At the more domestic level, the whole Owen family made good use of the otherwise unimaginable luxury that Tom could provide – access to free or very cheap rail travel. In Birkenhead this had enabled them to take regular family holidays (including in Ireland and Scarborough), while Susan Owen was able to sustain the family relationships and friendships which were crucial to her wellbeing.

Susan had found Birkenhead very different from the comforts and sheltered God-fearing household of her childhood in Oswestry. She retained profound memories of security and comfort in Plas Wilmot, the large and comfortable house built by her grandfather, which confirmed her father Edward Shaw's leading place in the town's commercial life. He had prospered as the owner of a successful ironmongery

Fig. 6 *Plas Wilmot, Oswestry. Susan's childhood home and the birthplace of Wilfred and his sister Mary.*

business, and as a magistrate and councillor who served a year as mayor of Oswestry, and was also Superintendent of St Oswald's Sunday School. Susan and her sisters were educated at home, with strong Methodist principles and Bible study, lessons in French, painting and playing the piano. Her only contact with the harshness of the wider world came through the misdeeds (particularly drink and gambling) of her only brother, another Edward, who eventually vanished to the United States.

No record survives of Susan's personal interests beyond her family and her church. Her most frequent visits were to her sister Emma Gunston, who was equally keenly attached to the Methodist beliefs and traditions of their childhood. First in Wimbledon and then at their comfortable house at Kidmore End near Reading, Emma was a constant source of support, particularly as Susan's general health declined. When he was old enough to travel unaccompanied, Wilfred also became a regular part of the Gunston household in his school holidays, and Emma's children became his closest friends and allies.

In 1907 Susan reached the age of 40 and has been described as quiet and affection-ate, with dark blue eyes and fine skin – and also as having an invincible belief in her God, and a very determined sense of purpose. Modest and reticent in company, and no doubt recalling her own secure childhood before various bereavements and tribulations, she seemed happiest inside her own house or close to home, where Mary grew to be her companion and household support. Both Susan and Tom were always concerned for their children's appearance and behaviour in public, and for their wellbeing.

When they married in 1891, Tom joined Susan in Plas Wilmot so she could continue caring for her now widowed father, Edward. Wilfred was born here in 1893, and Mary just over three years later. In his retirement, however, Edward Shaw lived off his capital, and at his death in 1897 he left the young family nothing but debts and despair. Bankruptcy was unavoidable, and Susan was left with no more than some household linen and bits of silver as mementoes of this vanished childhood. It was felt as a public humiliation, and for the rest of her life the house of her childhood remained in Susan's memory as a haven of comfort and quiet order that nothing else could quite match.

After the bankruptcy sale the couple moved to Cherry Orchard in Shrewsbury, not far from Tom's parents, to a new house in Canon Street where, as its first tenants, they had the name 'Wilmot' carved above the front door. Harold was born here later in the same year and Tom continued to work at Oswestry station, commuting daily by train from Shrewsbury. Their next move was to Birkenhead in 1900, very shortly before the birth of Colin, and at this stage Susan's general health began to decline – the consequence, perhaps, of three house-moves during their seven years in the city, and the demands of four young children on a very modest salary.

Tom found the nearby Shropshire countryside a delight after the intensely industrial working conditions in Birkenhead. Fully a man of the industrial age, he had greatly enjoyed his early experience of a sea-faring life as he worked his way out to India at the peak of the British Empire before returning to the land-bound life of a railway clerk and later station superintendent. Nothing in Harold's memoirs or Wilfred's letters show much sense of local pride and history, or awareness that Shrewsbury in its late medieval heyday was one of the country's largest towns, with its fine half-timbered houses and prosperous trade. The stone-built Old Market Hall in the central Square had been constructed to operate at the heart of the woollen trade: its great windows, impressive in themselves, showed off the merits of the local woollen goods to commercial traders from far and wide, including overseas. The town's later fame as one of the country's leading industrial centres of a hundred years earlier had declined, and it was now a typical provincial market town at the centre of a large rural county.

In 1907, the family must have wondered how life would develop in their new home town, knowing only that the railway was of great importance in their lives and prospects. There had once been an additional railway line in the town, based in the open ground close to the Abbey; but the Joint Railways (Tom's employers) had denied it full access to their network so that the vital final junction never completely materialised. In 1880 it became one of the very few Victorian railway lines in the country to cease operating.

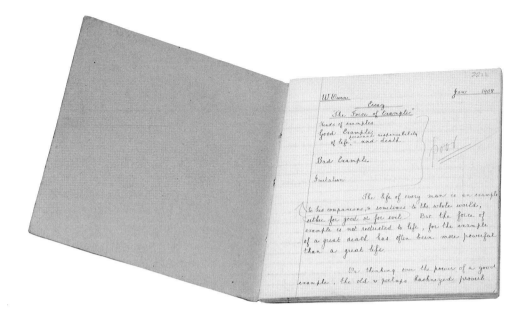

Fig. 7 *'The Force of Example' with a list of good and bad examples, from one of Wilfred's exercise books. It clearly did not impress his teacher (1908).*

For the two older boys, their education was presumably the most urgent concern. Wilfred's childhood was conventional for a modest, respectable and hard-working family, and he had advanced through Birkenhead Institute calmly and successfully, with an evident enthusiasm for learning. His good friendships included with the headmaster's son, and he had happily accompanied the family on farmhouse holidays in North Wales, sending some delightful letters home which showed his appreciation of the harsh landscape and perhaps the first stirrings of his poetic imagination. He was also, of course, a twelve-year-old boy exploring wild, Welsh hills, and there were setbacks, as described in a letter of mid-August 1905:

> *I have had a little bad luck. Up Moel Famma I lost my big fat knife I think. I am very sorry to say I broke the end of your umbrella. We tried to fish with the end of our rods in a tiny stream that runs into the Clwyd. I lent Alec a hook which he lost, & I lost my own, & cracked the tip end of my rod. I have bought a Picture Postcard for Harold which I hope to send tomorrow.*
>
> *With best love to all from Wilfred*

Wilfred's interests and achievements indicated future advances, and when the Owen family announced their imminent move to Shrewsbury it was proposed that he should board with the headmaster's household, so that he could remain at the Institute. However, Susan could not contemplate parting with her precious eldest son – the focus of her greatest love, attention and encouragement – and he travelled with the family to this new and unknown future.

Now nearly 14, Wilfred had probably gained the most from the family's seven years in Birkenhead, and he had reached the age when most children left school to earn their living. The move represented a considerable threat to a boy who was already dreaming of a literary life and wished above all to pursue his education. For him, the move to Shrewsbury represented the loss both of friends and a clear future, and everything would now depend on the possibilities available, and his own efforts. It was an awkward sense of committed purpose for a child in a family of modest means and no literary connections, but it would drive him through the challenging years of education ahead.

Harold, now ten, had spent a short time at the Institute with Wilfred, but both then and later he distinguished himself mainly by his apparent inability to learn. The outcome had been attempts at education marked by a series of confrontations, which Harold recorded in his memoirs as generally the result of other people misunderstanding his intentions, a liking for exploring the streets of Birkenhead on his own and a capacity for getting into fights. Although four years younger than Wilfred, Harold soon grew to be taller and stockier, a more substantial and impulsive figure as a child. He was always more physical in his approach to people or events, and enjoyed drawing, football and observation of the world around him.

Although Mary was the second child in the family, and 11 years old at the time of the family's move to Shrewsbury, she was so small and quiet that while the two brothers were often treated as a pair to be prepared for the outside world she remained at home. Colin, who was seven years old at the time of the move, was treated by all with love and tenderness, and concern for his health. Due to a weakness in his legs (probably rickets as the result of poor diet) he was obliged to wear heavy leg-irons for a long period during his childhood. He appears in Wilfred's letters mostly as the object of very fond elder-brotherly concern, gentle teasing and affection, with occasional advice or warnings. Wilfred also, rather touchingly, tried in later years to steer his mother away from what he perceived as her overly protective or serious-minded concern for Colin's physical and spiritual wellbeing – perhaps a reflection of his feelings about how he himself had been treated in adolescence.

Fig. 8 (overleaf) *Excavating the station yard in 1903, to improve access and create the present ground floor of the station building. Soil is dug out with hand tools and loaded into carts, while cabs line up for fares.*

The Shrewsbury of 1907 – the year the Owens arrived in the town – differed from the town of today in many regards, not least in the spreading development of roads and suburbs. It is still difficult to reach the centre of Shrewsbury without being aware of the River Severn, tightly wound round the old heart of the town, but what is much less easily seen is the next large bend downstream, below the English Bridge, where a long stretch of water runs past the castle and the station before curving round in a long, irregular loop away from the town. In that earlier era much of the ground contained within this wide river curve consisted of low-lying meadows and farmland, to an extent very difficult to envisage from the streets of the twenty-first-century town. The banks of the river held clumps of willow and bushes, and occasional small islands or mud-banks emerged when the river ran low.

Proximity to the river was a great attraction and held no fears for the Owens, since Tom had already insisted that his children should be first-class swimmers. This process had taken place in Birkenhead Public Baths, using methods strongly criticised by Susan, to ensure that they should be able to swim the width of the baths at the age of six, and the full length by the time of their eighth birthday. This included a ceremony, partway through the course of learning, when Tom would fix a date for his own invented ritual: on this day, the 'victim' would be taken to the deep end of the pool, picked up by Tom and thrown in from the middle diving board. Tom would then dive in and rescue the candidate. Notwithstanding Susan's disapproval, Tom gave repeated

Figs. 9 & 10 *Shrewsbury Baths, Priory Road. Built in 1887 for Queen Victoria's Golden Jubilee, the large building displays municipal pride with its decorative entrance and coat of arms over the door (c.1900).*

and detailed descriptions ahead of this immersion, with much emphasis on the courage required. For Harold it was a thoroughly unhappy introduction to swimming, but Wilfred learned quickly and became adept; although slightly built, he was a strong and athletic child and later became a fearless and expert horseman. Whether or not Mary was taught to swim in the same way is not recorded, but it seems improbable.

Shrewsbury appeared a great deal greener and calmer than the industrial urgency of Birkenhead – even before any of the Owens discovered their rural surroundings outside the town. The two roads stretching out from the Abbey to the north-east, Underdale and Monkmoor, carried very little traffic; they led only to a few houses along the riverbank, farms and scattered buildings, before petering out as farm tracks through the fields and down to the riverbank. The Owens would be living in one of the quietest suburbs of a town that was comfortably distant from the modern industrial world.

Without a road bridge outside the central town area between Montford Bridge upstream and Atcham downstream, these loops of the river could be crossed only by ferry. In the case of Monkmoor Road, its final stretch led to a ferry providing a practical link between Shrewsbury and the village of Uffington, which was otherwise accessible only via several miles of roadway. This ferry, the village and church, and the flanks of Haughmond Hill beyond became a great resource for the Owen family, and for Harold in particular.

In 1907 the pleasures of the riverbanks and the countryside beyond the suburb were therefore easy to explore from Cleveland Place in Underdale Road, the house the Owens rented near Tom's parents. It stood at the centre of a block of three dwellings – a miniature terrace which turned the corner, with tight terraces running up Cleveland Street behind and a few larger individual houses alongside it. Although the houses built here from the 1880s onwards, and in the more precisely planned streets of Cherry Orchard, appear to have been planned to a comprehensive design in the same style and brickwork, the sections of terracing or pairs of semi-detached houses were generally built as small, separate developments over several decades. The larger house built at the end of most streets might represent the developer's own residence, but otherwise the cohesive overall appearance quickly attracted families

Fig. 11 *The Owens' house at Cleveland Place.*

who could afford to rent them. Railway officials like Tom Owen were typical of these new suburban residents, although many railway workers were more likely to live in the smaller terrace houses that spread out north of the station.

Despite its height and solid substance, the tall Cleveland Place house was not large. Local records show that bathrooms were added at the rear of the houses in the early 1900s, but the attic bedroom, which was shared by Wilfred and Harold, had no form of lighting or possibility of heating. Harold writes of watching his older brother studying for long hours by candlelight, huddled in blankets for warmth. Writing some years later, a neighbour described seeing the constant light in this

Fig. 12 *Underdale ferry: a convenient river crossing for Tom Owen between home and the station (1907).*

bedroom while Wilfred laboured over his homework, and his morning appearance as he staggered out hastily under his burden of school-books. Perhaps Wilfred's preference for solitary study in attic bedrooms, fostered in this and their next edge-of-town house, was reflected some years later in Scarborough when his army posting enabled him to choose a splendid tower bedroom for himself, chilly but looking far out to sea.

The Owens' neighbours represented a community that could be recognised in many other towns, with homes for shopkeepers and office workers, factory foremen and craftsmen, senior clerks and owners of small businesses, and a few professional men. In 1916 the town directory listed a range of professions or occupations among residents in streets off Monkmoor Road. These included surveyor, insurance agent, inspector, builder, outfitter, farmer, ironmonger, ordnance survey clerk, engine driver and clerk in one street; a manager, clerks, a piano tuner and a carpenter in another. Harold was very disparaging about the type of resident in the residential streets of terraces and houses between Underdale Road and Monkmoor Road, and described 'slatternly' women, rough children, jeers and unkempt style. This constant approach may have been part of his need to show how life had changed for the worse for the Owen family since leaving Susan's beloved Plas Wilmot; he tended to favour his father against his mother in general family life, but in descriptions that often tended to reflect harshly on Tom Owen and his provision for his family.

One of the many ferries along the town stretch of river was conveniently close for Tom Owen to reach the station, and enabled him to come home regularly for lunch. For centuries the riverbanks had been an essential part of the town's working life, long before their present-day use for sport and leisure, from rowing to fishing or walking along the banks. The river was a natural route for carrying goods of all kinds in and out of the town, with slipways, warehouses and wharves – some buildings and traces of which still survive – serving commercial life along the banks; but it was also well-used at this time for sport and leisure, including regattas, picnic outings or simple rowing-boat excursions up or down the river.

Some of the modern open spaces by the river relate to this busy past, while across the up-and-down town centre a series of churches and their surrounding open spaces marks their life in local parishes and contributes to the distinctive skyline to be enjoyed from the English Bridge. The spire of St Mary's, visible from far around, with St Alkmund's and St Julian's close by at the heart of the old town, is followed by the ruins of old St Chad's as the final trace of a large medieval establishment. The largest space of all, the Quarry, slopes down to the river from the 'new' St Chad's, built in 1792. In contrast to the tight street pattern, the park provides an avenue of trees along the river bank, and broad stretches of green, with an enclosed, sunken garden at the centre, on the site of an early stone quarry.

How different it was from Birkenhead and the River Mersey! Liverpool's great maritime seaway was a vigorous setting, open to the world and the Empire with shipping constantly on the move and all the vivid sights, smells and ideas from every imaginable port; while in Shrewsbury the River Severn curved decorously round the tight-packed streets and alleys of the town centre. It was still constantly busy, however, with ferries crossing the river at several points, and boats for hire for exercise or pleasure. There were dramas to see too, for heavy rain away to the west in the Welsh mountains would bring torrents of turbulent brown water sweeping down, bearing debris of all sorts, frothing under the old stone bridges and flooding out over the banks. The high days of the river's use as the main route to the outside world were long gone now, and the steady traffic of barges and sailing boats carrying goods and supplies of all kinds to and from workshops, factories and traders had yielded to the railways and carters' wagons spreading out across the county.

A century before the Owens' time in Shrewsbury, the town had been at the heart of heavy engineering and manufacturing, but this focus of invention and creation had ebbed away to other and larger industrial regions. What remained was the market town at this important river crossing at the centre of a large rural county and its traditional local activities. On the English and Welsh bridges, traffic was crowded, livestock being driven to market could easily block the way, and the river was a clear mark of the shift from the outer suburbs and open countryside to the picturesque old town.

It was accepted, beyond any need for comment, that town life was generally dirty, noisy, crowded and frequently unhealthy, with pollution a constant feature of air, ground and water. With a persistent and pervasive atmosphere of smoke, smells, grimy air from coal fires, forges and steam power affecting buildings, residents and pedestrians in most towns, the more prosperous residents would often prefer to live out in cleaner country air – provided they could find and afford a good site with a reliable source of water.

An extreme example of industrial damage in Shrewsbury was that caused by Thomas Burr, who in the early 1800s moved his lead works establishment from its site within the bridges to an old linen-weaving factory on the outer river bank. He became extremely successful, often using the output of the local Snailbeach lead mines in the production of sheet lead, shot and lead piping. The air pollution from his factory caused many complaints, and an official governmental report admonished the Borough of Shrewsbury in 1854 over the clouds of foul-smelling smoke that scattered the area with poisonous lead. The borough was slow to take action, and for many years the ground was considered too heavily contaminated for agricultural or housing use.

Not many activities were as harmful as the lead-making, but when the river ran low, as in the summer months, banks emerged in areas such as the bend between the

Fig. 13 *Flooding by Shrewsbury Abbey. The profile of these buildings is still clearly recognisable.*

Rea Brook and the English Bridge, or around the piers of the bridges. As the river rounded the bend and ran slow, these banks, covered with accumulated weeds and rubbish, became polluted and foul-smelling. By the time this was added to airborne pollution from workshops and factories, the dirty smoke from engines of all kinds, trains, and livestock being driven to and from the market on Smithfield, or to the butchers' shops and abattoirs, it was often no pleasure to walk along riverside streets or across the bridges.

The Owens were fortunate in arriving after Shrewsbury's drainage and sewerage problems had mainly been resolved, for in 1901 full-scale drainage and sanitation became a reality with the opening of the Coleham Pumping Station. This is still a local landmark, which opens its doors on special days for visitors to see the magnificent engines under steam. Elaborate construction work was required for the new system, which included tunnelling under the river, and two steam-powered pumping engines were linked to a vast new treatment centre far down the Monkmoor Road. A few years later the weir was built downstream from the railway bridge to maintain more consistent river levels, although flooding persisted as a recognised feature of the town, invading riverside streets and cellars. It was a regular and damaging local event, dramatic and, on rare occasions, even encroaching inside the Abbey.

Family life for the Owens settled down. Although Susan was reserved by nature, and heavily engaged in her household activities, the Owens gained some good friendships. Local neighbours were important, and it was an excellent area for the family to become quietly known and appreciated. Susan's established habit of visiting her sister Emma Gunston was followed in due course by Wilfred or the whole family together. Reference to these increasingly frequent absences from home of either Susan or Wilfred recurs constantly throughout the large collection of Wilfred's letters to his mother, reporting on activities either at home or with the Gunstons (unfortunately none of Susan's letters have survived). Evidently the warm and supportive atmosphere in her sister's house was helpful for her wellbeing in every respect.

During one of Susan's visits to her sister, in January 1908, Wilfred, by now 15, wrote to her about daily life at home. By now he enjoyed writing chatty and entertaining letters, with a note of gently mocking affection for members of the family ('the Mansell game', referred to here, was the delicate question of how many books he was permitted to buy at a bookshop in the town):

Fig. 14 *Shrewsbury weir under construction. Completed in 1911, the weir between Underdale and Castle Walk was part of the project to sustain high river levels and modernise Shrewsbury's water system.*

Father is cleaning the bath this evening! with paraffin oil. The smell is permeating the whole house most abominably (snorts). As I said yesterday the Mansell game is beginning again (ferocious glares). We have lots more books to get (redoubled glares & snorts) but we have already got some …

Harold seems likely to have known the town quite well, although his memoirs cannot be used as the basis for a full modern understanding of the community. This later record of his own life is based on his vivid but sometimes unreliable memories of family life and his generally unrewarding school life, but the strongest image of the family's relationship with their surroundings is of conventional manners and behaviour within the household, and informal sociability with local friends. Their houses in Birkenhead had not offered much outdoor space where children might play safely, and from a young age Wilfred had frequently been deputed to take Mary and Harold through the closely terraced streets to dreary urban waste ground which to Harold sometimes seemed vaguely threatening. Now there was the river and its banks and meadows, with fresh air and accessible countryside – far more welcoming than the industrial Mersey. Tom loved bird-watching and sport, or simply being out of doors, and enjoyed taking Wilfred and Harold out to explore. Although Wilfred was not keen on the very early morning departure that Tom required, the sense of being at home in the natural world which underlies much of his poetry – the terrible contrast between the landscape and what the war did to it – must have its foundation, in part, from these outings.

Susan, who had disliked Birkenhead, could perhaps rediscover in Shrewsbury some aspects of life that reminded her a little of her home town, Oswestry. As part of local life the names of important local people, such as her father had been in his active working life, would become known. In the family's first two years in the town, 1907 and 1908, the Mayor of Shrewsbury was Benjamin Blower, an upholsterer; and no doubt at some point they noticed the substantial commercial building near Shrewsbury station, with its still-surviving wide archway and the name 'Blowers Repository' carved in stone above it. It was the sign of a substantial and confident family establishment, with its main premises in Pride Hill, the town's central 'spine' of shops where the name can still be seen high up on one of the surviving façades near the top of the street. Other mayors in recent years had included a tailor, a malt-ster and a brewer; while in the years ahead there would be a Justice of the Peace, a gentleman (that is, prosperous and well-educated enough not to need a profession or employment) and, through three of the war years, a solicitor.

One great advantage for Tom Owen was the small railway 'set-down' halt beside Underdale Road, very close to their first house in Shrewsbury. Until it closed in 1912, it was a convenient halt for residents to leave the train without crossing the river into the main station; and as the Assistant Superintendent at the station he could use it to take him directly into or out of his place of work. From this halt, Underdale Road led back to the much older Abbey terrain and a row of tall, early nineteenth-century houses, Holywell Terrace, which faced Horse Fair (once part of the Abbey's extensive lands). In the long period after Henry VIII's Dissolution of the Monasteries had dispossessed the Abbey of its wealth, the monastic community was broken up and the monks and lay brothers disappeared into secular life. Over time the ground became a mixture of market-place, cottages, builders' yards and open space used for fairs and markets, and later a children's playground. Two substantial houses from the seventeenth and eighteenth centuries still define the corner leading round to the Abbey, both facing the substantial bulk of the Abbey itself and reflecting the more prosperous times in earlier centuries. A row of almshouses by the church, rebuilt in Tudor style in 1820, is a surviving reminder of the medieval tradition of charity and care – evidence too of the medieval Drapers' Guild, which continues to uphold this ancient charitable good work in the form of modern accommodation very close to the Abbey.

The immediate area evidently felt comfortable and safe for the Owens, and the children's upbringing encouraged them to be open, friendly and respectful. After the move to Monkmoor Road in 1910, the Ragge family, living almost next door, became particular friends. Their two children, John and Mary, matched Wilfred and Harold pretty well in age and often accompanied them in their exploration of the countryside. By the time that Wilfred left school and moved on in the world, Colin was old enough to join in too. The Ragge and Owen parents were also good friends – a bond that no doubt deepened later when their sons were killed in action: John Ragge in September 1918 and Wilfred Owen a few weeks later in November. Many years later the link was renewed between the Ragges and Colin's family, and Mary Ragge recorded her memories of the Owen family in her childhood in conversations and written notes.

In the early years of the twentieth century, the riverbank outside the town centre, which was much less built over than it would be in later decades, provided considerable variety. The substantial bulk of Shrewsbury School's main building, with its chequered history (fever hospital, prison in the Napoleonic wars, orphanage, workhouse, and eventually the heart of a large fee-paying school), still stands on a steep green bank, facing the Quarry. This view of privilege, more than almost any other element of the town, would later stir Wilfred to uncomfortable thoughts about his own background – his education, and other differences between his background and that of wealthier families as he encountered adult life outside Shrewsbury.

Further round the river curve, towards the English Bridge, came the final traces of Shrewsbury's early industrial significance in Old Coleham and Longden Coleham. A group of gifted and creative men included three generations of the Carline family,

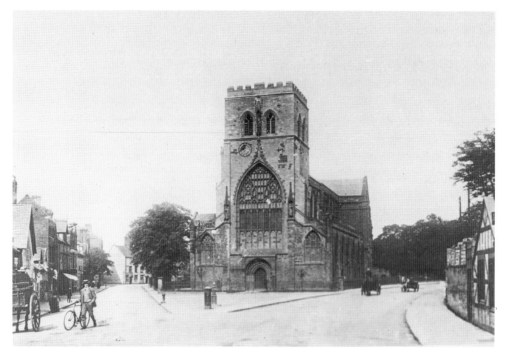

Fig. 15 *Shrewsbury Abbey from the south-west, showing a man in a straw boater and wheeling a bicycle. Local traffic is horse-drawn, and the Victorian pillar box in front of the church is still in use.*

the great road-builder and engineer Thomas Telford and William Hazledine (whose own house still survives close to the bridge, on the town side) as they designed and built roads, bridges, canal locks and aqueducts. Together they turned the town and the River Severn into a centre of industrial invention and growth. Hazledine had his foundry in Coleham in the late 1790s and early 1800s, between the Crown Inn and the Greyfriars footbridge, and the products transported along the river included such landmarks as the chains for the Menai Suspension Bridge, one of the wonders of the early nineteenth-century era.

In Longden Coleham, the site of the church of St Barnabas and the area behind was once occupied by the local Yeomanry drill hall and riding school, where working horses, wagons and carts of all kinds mingled with military training and horsemen. Streets of small, terraced houses provided minimal accommodation for crowded families on the ground that is now the Carline Fields complex, and the whole area was a network of narrow streets, passages and public houses for some of the town's poorest residents. In the nineteenth century a Sunday school was established in Hulbert's 'cotton manufactory' and the nature of the area came into wider focus. Although it is no longer linked to the riverbank, the plain building facing Longden Coleham (between the Crown Inn and the Greyfriars footbridge) represents the final evidence of this industrial past.

Fig. 16 *Lowcock's Foundry, Longden Coleham, close to the Greyfriars footbridge and seen here from across the Severn. Built in the 1820s by William Hazledine, it became celebrated. It was demolished in 1934.*

By 1907 the area was in decline. The heavier, physically-demanding activity – held responsible for at least some of the many public houses in the area – was dying out and factories were closing, moving or being used as shops. The heavily-populated narrow streets and alleys were suffering overcrowding, diminishing employment and cramped, decaying and insanitary cottages on the ground that is now Carline Fields. One may safely suppose that all of this area would have been forbidden ground for the Owen family.

The substantial, red sandstone Abbey building itself had once held considerable significance as a separate independent community, with great power during the Middle Ages. Its dissolution in 1540 marked the loss of its wealth and political influence. Much of the stone gradually disappeared as it was taken for building in the area, and what had been refectory, fish-ponds and gardens became overgrown or used for short-term ventures. In 1836, Thomas Telford's new road ran brutally close to the Abbey, carving through the ruins and leaving it isolated from the surviving remains of its extensive grounds. The introduction of the railway system in the mid-nineteenth century required the construction of the large viaduct carrying the main line south towards Ludlow, Hereford and South Wales, which also struck across this area of uncertain use.

Beside the river, the garden and open terrain next to Carline's house were a part of the Abbey grounds where the monks' medicinal plants were grown, according to local legend. However, by the Owens' time it was hemmed in by the solid barrier of the railway embankment, and in 1910 it became the ground for the town's football club – said to be the only one in the country with a boat standing by during matches, to retrieve balls kicked into the river. On the south side of Abbey Foregate, a variety of enterprises invaded the abandoned land with a shifting pattern of occupancy. Travelling fairs appeared from time to time with entertainments and shows, circuses and, on one occasion, a display involving genuine gunboats to re-enact Lord Kitchener's expedition to Khartoum.

At least two major enterprises made longer-term use of this land. One was the light railway line, grandly named 'The Potteries, Shrewsbury and North Wales Railway', which resulted in the opening of a station in 1866 on former Abbey land, the demolition of a large Abbey building, the draining of the millpond by the brook and the clearance of a garden. By 1880 it had become one of the very few Victorian railways which ceased to operate, and other enterprises made use of its premises and

Fig. 17 *Aerial acrobatics in the Quarry, in front of St Chad's. An admiring group watches a public display of free entertainment on a sunny day (early twentieth century).*

Fig. 18 *Smiths with their anvil and forge in Beeches Lane, a busy town centre workshop, with the men wearing heavy, protective aprons. Tools and horseshoes hang on the wall ready for use (c.1900).*

land until it underwent an optimistic revival in 1911. The second and more successful venture was established beside the old railway track, and set somewhat further from the road past the Abbey: this, the Midland Railway Carriage and Wagon Company, became a substantial local employer, building railway and tram coaches for London and export from the late 1800s. Although Shrewsbury itself never acquired a tram network, this was the first national tram-making factory, and in 1894 it had sent a fleet of new 'Two-Horse Forty-Seat' tramcars for Glasgow Corporation Tramways.

The works closed in 1912, but in the First World War, in a development unthinkable back in 1907, the old factory buildings were used as a prisoner-of-war camp. The establishment, its German occupants and the garden and washing lines they set up were clearly visible to neighbours and passing traffic. Through it all, one building survived from the old Abbey establishment, and is still in use. It is thought to have been the monks' infirmary and is now (perhaps suitably in the twenty-first century) a centre for environmental protection. Otherwise, for many years the area remained ill-defined, with stretches of waste ground around builders' yards, commercial depots and empty premises. For local children of several generations it was known generally as 'Back of the Sheds' – a vivid name for unused buildings and unkempt ground.

Fig. 19 *W.B. Walkers, printers and stationers, Fish Street. Staff outside the premises, including men and women, managers, apprentices and errand boys (c.1910).*

From a different point of view, the major redevelopment initiated by Telford and his road confirmed Abbey Foregate as the grandest way into the town, and in the early 1900s it was broad and tree-lined, with houses and terraces of all sizes and styles from the preceding centuries, facing the road or set back on the gentle slope up to St Giles and Sutton. At the top of the slope the tall Column monument was a prominent landmark (taller and wider than Nelson's Column in Trafalgar Square), built to honour a local man for his achievements in the Napoleonic wars: Rowland Hill – the first Viscount Hill – a much-loved and successful general from an important local family. Close to the Column, the traditional church of St Giles occasionally offered Tom Owen a welcome alternative place of worship when others of the family preferred a more evangelical style in a town church.

As Shrewsbury's early industrial inventiveness and activity declined, the town was spared the sweeping redevelopment and new factory-inspired growth of nineteenth-century Britain, and retained its cramped medieval street pattern, churches, markets, workshops and trade, with brick or half-timbered buildings of all sizes and styles. Curious and inexplicable ancient street names survived. Commerce, churches and chapels shared the streets with private houses, large and small, with narrow alleys, or 'shuts', running through and between them. From grand houses to tiny rooms behind shops, living in basements or up into the attics, the town was full of people, noise and busy-ness.

Many years later, Harold's record of the Owens' life in Birkenhead (when he was a very young child) depicted their houses there over nearly seven years as dismal, cramped, awkward places, with dangers lurking outside. These descriptions seem at odds with the houses themselves and their locations, all still surviving in a pleasant area and not among slums or terrace rows around the docks. Harold's main pleasure seems to have been to explore the streets, where he was proud of his ability to stand his ground in confrontations with local boys.

Shrewsbury, in contrast, was small and sufficiently compact to retain its awareness of the surrounding landscape – as befitted the county town with easy access to the surrounding fields and hills. Shropshire's landscape, of hills and hollows and stretches of moorland resembling the Welsh hills not far off, with few towns, scattered villages and many remote farms and hamlets, preserved its own local differences. The Owen children learned from their father to appreciate landscape and wildlife, and Wilfred in particular learned at school about the geology and botany of this distinctive region. These elements defined the county's way of life, and the hardness of life in remote farms; agriculture and the rural life predominated and dictated the pattern of life as well as urban trades and commerce.

2   SCHOOL DAYS

much happier in every way

ALONG with the rest of Britain, Shrewsbury changed profoundly in the nineteenth century. The town walls had all but disappeared, leaving a few inconspicuous roadside traces, but as the Industrial Revolution spread across the country the town expanded across the river into working and residential areas. Thomas Telford remodelled the medieval castle and used Shrewsbury as his base for many years during his career, building roads, bridges and canals; and Shropshire's early manufacturing and industrialisation developed in the foundries, factories and workshops in the Coleham area, along the Severn and by the Rea Brook.

On the other side of town, crafts and trades developed on both sides of the Welsh Bridge, with quays, a boat-yard and workshops on the outer bank and the livestock market, tannery and associated trades along the inner bank. Near both bridges, forges, metal-working, repair shops of all kinds and associated commerce were lively, noisy and dirty – with the associated crowds, materials, smells and rough company generally avoided by the middle or more prosperous classes.

Although the town centre itself escaped the major Victorian remodelling that affected many others, the Severn was still busy with a multiplicity of ferries and river craft, while the canal network brought in bulk freight of all kinds. The railway system spread across the whole country, imposing itself on the countryside and changing the townscape. Shrewsbury station extended its platforms across the River Severn to cater for its increasing activity, with its freight and passenger services arriving and leaving in six different directions from this important provincial centre.

The modern English Bridge dates from the mid-1920s, when it was rebuilt, using most of the same stone. It replaced its predecessor with a lower gradient – since it

Fig. 20 (overleaf) *Aerial view of the town and river looking north-west. The English Bridge, demolished and rebuilt in 1927, leads into Wyle Cop and up into town close to the tower of St Julian's. The spires of St Mary's and St Alkmund's stand out, with a large circular water tower between them. In the foreground is the Coleham Pumping Station. The ornate rooftop and tower to upper left identifies the old Victorian market hall.*

Fig. 21 *The English Bridge with the river at low water before the weir was built to raise water levels, and the Rea Brook in the foreground. The bridge was reconstructed in 1925–27.*

was no longer necessary to allow for sailing craft – and was much wider, to ease the constant delays and traffic tangles, particularly when livestock was driven to market or butchers' shops. The first medieval stone bridge, which lasted until the mid-eighteenth century, had extended on to a wooden structure of roadway and arches, known as the Monks' Bridge, across what was then a distinct, separate island and into the Abbey grounds. This island was absorbed into the present-day Abbey Foregate area as part of the main bridge reconstruction in the 1770s, which was established by the first of three generations of Carlines. The same family built the dignified house by the bridge, which from 1899 onwards was used to house the Technical School.

Between them, the Carlines, Thomas Telford and William Hazledine were responsible for a tremendous amount of innovation, engineering and building, here and – particularly in the case of Telford – throughout the country. It was Telford who rebuilt the ruins of Shrewsbury Castle on behalf of the local Member of Parliament, and turned it into the castellated house that now stands above the station. In the 1830s his new road, part of the great London to Holyhead route, radically changed the area round the Abbey as it swept through the remaining monastic ruins and close to the church itself. In the 1880s, however, the Abbey itself was considerably restored and refurbished out of a bequest of £10,000 from a local resident, Mrs Hannah Juson. Although nothing could restore it to its previous power and status, it was a reassuring restatement of its history and enduring place in local worship.

By the time the Owens reached Shrewsbury, this area around the remaining ruins to the south of the Abbey had taken on a shifting role in local activities. We may suppose that it would have been more or less 'out of bounds' to Wilfred and Harold as they explored their surroundings – although, when Harold became a keen art student, he was introduced by his father to Bickerton's builders' yard close to the Abbey, to enjoy the serious business of discussing and buying the best kind of board that he could afford for his paintings.

Over many decades during the nineteenth century, the area gradually changed its appearance as the earlier realignment of water-courses and roads on this side of the river was followed by two railway ventures. The first, and most enduring, was the long embankment carrying the new Shrewsbury to Hereford line in the 1850s. This cut off the view of the river; and a decade later the ill-fated Potteries, Shrewsbury and North-West Wales railway line set up its terminus station next to Abbey Foregate. Between these two, and stretching away from Telford's road, the land filled up with tracks, sidings, workshops, a brick depot and the Midlands Railway Carriage & Wagon Company's premises.

The whole of the area beside Abbey Foregate is now in public use. The local railway heritage trust uses the surviving light railway ticket office, while the sharp angle of the one-way road system has a fine Queen Anne house next to the former Shrewsbury Abbey Infirmary. The latter was once used as a maltings, and a few tantalising archaeological remains lie beneath the modern car park. These two buildings now house

Fig. 22 *Bickerton's & Bullock's Works after a fire, with some of the walls still standing among the piles of timber and rubble. Firemen and labourers work against the backdrop of the old Abbey 'Infirmary' building (1906).*

Shropshire's wildlife trust. Beyond the car park and stretching down the modern road beside the embankment, a large supermarket and other commercial premises occupy the former Abbey gardens and mill premises along the Rea Brook.

Once the Owen family was established in Cleveland Place, and with Tom securely employed at Shrewsbury station, the children's education was one of the family's first concerns. Mary, the second child (but always somewhat in the shadow of her brothers), was enrolled in a small private school nearby, where Colin, the baby of the family, would join her in due course. The proprietor, Miss Goodwin, became known to the Owens as 'Goodie', and in the years ahead was a trusted and supportive friend of the family. In time she came to the house to teach Wilfred, Mary and Colin to play the piano, advise Wilfred on his French and offer useful professional advice on Harold's education. Susan later took on a small infants' class for her in the family home.

Wilfred and Harold both posed their own educational challenges, and even allowing for Harold's very personal memory and point of view as seen in his memoirs, the differences between their aptitudes were striking. Harold presented an apparently insoluble problem: he seemed impervious to formal education, and his somewhat impulsive character quite frequently – and, in his eyes, entirely unjustly – landed him in trouble with teachers and his fellow-pupils. He had followed Wilfred at Birkenhead Institute, but with a markedly lower level of success, as he found conventional learning almost impossible. In a later generation he would probably have been identified as suffering from the then-unrecognised condition of dyslexia. In his own account of his childhood, he tells of confusion, willingness on his part followed by a lack of rapport with his teachers, and a readiness to use his physical strength in the face of adult incomprehension or irritation. Although he loved drawing and observation of the world around him, his difficulty in conventional learning was genuinely disabling.

Given the family's modest income, it was decided that a regular, free elementary school would be most suitable for Harold, and Tom duly entered his son at what he felt would be a suitable establishment, somewhere on the far side of the town. As an uncertain newcomer, Harold found both the school and the headmaster daunting, but set off alone for his first appointed day. Perhaps characteristically, but also understandably in an unfamiliar town, he lost his way, arrived late and was met with what he felt was hostility and unwelcoming fellow-pupils. When he arrived home dishevelled, tired and frightened, his explanation of being set upon by a group of boys, first in the school playground and then on some waste ground at the end of the day, was met with his mother's alarm and his father's irritation. It is impossible to know how much this may be an exaggerated description of the school, or how typical of the period.

Harold's dismay at the other boys' disturbing behaviour and the school as a whole was treated with disbelief. He felt, then and later, that Susan's response to unpleasant truths was to disregard them. As he recorded in his memoirs, he found his mother's attitude unhelpful: she implied that it was not his place to question his attendance at the school, which was ordained by God and he must therefore bear it with patience. The frequent injunction that 'God will provide' struck Harold in particular as inadequate in the face of questions and problems, and he clearly felt that, in this case at least, God was somewhat misguided. Nonetheless, he remained at the school for some time, having won himself protection from his fellow-pupils through his strength and ability to fight (acquired in the streets of Birkenhead). He also realised that if he sat still and did not fidget, the teachers would leave him to dream his own thoughts.

In both Birkenhead and Shrewsbury, Harold's memoirs frequently describe unattractive and threatening streets. His new schoolmates were a similar challenge, so that he did not make friends among his fellow-pupils. Many of Shrewsbury's narrow passages and alleys were genuinely disturbing to carefully-nurtured children, badly lit, overcrowded and often threatening. With his mother's constant memories of her own background and admonitions of good behaviour, Harold felt that the Owen family was always rightly concerned to preserve its dignity and superior style.

No doubt Susan and Tom despaired of this difficult boy and his apparent inability to get along with school life, while his struggles brought down earnest exhortations on his head for future good behaviour and acceptance. Amidst all this unhappiness, Harold found one teacher whose explanations made sense to him. We do not know her name, but her teaching of arithmetic brought him pleasure and understanding. Harold's talents lay in drawing and design (as would appear in later years), and the management of numbers to achieve a clear and correct answer intrigued and pleased him.

School education was compulsory until the age of 12, and the great majority of the nation's children left education at that point to earn their living. Now nearly 14, Wilfred was a very different character from Harold and the challenge that he represented for his parents was closely related to the potential cost of his continuing education and plans for his ultimate future. He had responded enthusiastically to the regular academic syllabus and atmosphere at Birkenhead Institute, embarking on a good general education and extending his imagination as well as his knowledge.

There was certainly no problem with his aptitude or willingness: by the age of 13 or 14, he was writing essays which reflected widely-held attitudes on Britain's position in the world in the early 1900s. The implication was that the nation must have good leaders with the right moral attitudes for their natural destiny in the world. One surviving essay shows the teacher begging for an initial outline but including a paragraph (marked 'VG') in which the young pupil extolled the virtues of liberty, freedom, the greatness of England, duty, the power of example and the need to labour selflessly for the country. Another essay, entitled 'The Force of Example' (*see Fig. 7, page 10*), received a (double underlined) 'poor' comment for its initial outline. The need for a clear structure was emphasised – and in view of his later intense attention to poetic structure, it was evidently well understood. The expectations and assumptions of imperial, Edwardian Britain are all present and, from what little we can glimpse of his parents' attitudes, this approach would surely be endorsed at home. Susan's insistence on Christian faith, duty to one's fellow-man and steady patience confirmed it, with the importance of bearing witness and pursuing the higher duty.

Susan was also determined to support her favourite child's talents and enthusiasm. She recognised his intellectual ability and thirst for wider knowledge (and lack of obvious practical aptitudes) and wanted above all to foster his literary instincts, to take his place in adult life as 'an educated man'. The style and expense of Shrewsbury School, prominent on the high river-bank opposite the Quarry park, was unthinkable – a fact of life accepted without discussion; and although Tom visited several private fee-paying establishments which claimed to educate 'the sons of gentlemen', he vetoed as 'inadequate' the only one of these which Susan and Wilfred found attractive.

Eventually, and after much debate, Tom's enquiries and investigations provided a

Fig. 23 *The Technical School garden as Wilfred Owen would have known it, with the spire of the United Reform Church visible beyond. John Carline's former house and gardens beside the English Bridge occupied part of the former Abbey gardens.*

Fig. 24 *Carline's House seen from Coleham Head, with the English Bridge to the left (c.1930). Wilfred Owen knew this house as the Shrewsbury Borough Technical School.*

solution which had the added advantage of being close to home: the Borough Technical School which now occupied John Carline's house at the junction of the English Bridge, Abbey Foregate and Coleham Head. Worship and education were clustered together here, with the bulk of the Abbey nearby, and a large National School linked to the Congregational Church.

This prominent building with its tall spire by the bridge, now the United Reformed Church, occupies the site of what was once a substantial and well-known inn. Complete with stabling and workshop, it served travellers and local workers. The premises included a reliable source of clean water (a great asset), and the inn was a useful stopping-point for both river and road traffic with all the associations of its trade. The horse-drawn barges and river craft of every kind, sailing or under tow – sometimes for many miles – were a steady source of business; the road itself brought coachmen and their passengers, and horses that needed stabling or care. Coachmen and bargees could refresh themselves, and the industrial foundries, factories and workshops close at hand in Longden Coleham provided plenty of custom.

A local woman, Mrs Julia Wightman, whose husband was vicar of St Alkmund's Church, was an ardent activist in the cause of temperance, and the evangelical fervour which swept the country during the nineteenth century. With her support and encouragement the Congregationalist community raised funds, bought the inn site and built their substantial and imposing church there to provide a different kind of comfort and support in the local community. It opened its doors in 1862 and later joined the United Reformed Church community of faith.

The Technical School in Carline House on the Abbey Foregate side of the bridge – generally known as 'the Technical' – had extended buildings and gardens stretching back along the riverside. It offered a surprising range of education under no fewer than three separate headings. Apart from its immediate technical and commercial courses, it housed the borough's Art School and, most relevant in Wilfred's case, the Pupil-Teacher Centre. These Centres, set up across the country, were designed to provide a suitable academic education for children whose parents could not afford to pay high fees but who were bright enough to merit secondary education at the nation's expense. This was not for philanthropic reasons but to produce the steady stream of teachers needed for the 'board' schools that provided free obligatory primary education.

The Head of the Technical School, Mr Timpany, concentrated much of the entire establishment's funds on the teacher-training side of the establishment – to the extent that an official rebuke reached him, complaining that insufficient attention was being paid to the school's practical syllabus. The Timpanys lived in Underdale Road, not far from the Owens, and they became family friends (much as Wilfred had been a close friend of his headmaster's son in Birkenhead).

Pupil-teachers received a good education, and worked extremely hard to achieve it. They first had to be considered academically capable of passing the demanding matriculation examination, and in effect be prepared to commit themselves to elementary school teaching. In return for this, fees were minimal or not charged; but in their two final years the workload for PTA pupils was doubled, as they spent some two days each week on practical teaching in their allotted junior school.

Wilfred could not deny the impractical prospects for his enduring literary ambitions, and recognised that the type of future that he craved probably depended on achieving a university degree. His parents were prepared to support him through his secondary education, but the cost of a degree course thereafter was clearly beyond their financial prospects. His only chance lay in achieving a sufficiently high pass at matriculation to win a scholarship. It was a daunting prospect for the ambitious pupil, and Wilfred was given clear warnings of the unpalatable future of a full professional life spent in elementary teaching (both the head teacher, Mr Timpany, and his wife emphasised this to the Owens). However, 'the Technical' employed some excellent teachers, Wilfred was a determined pupil, and despite the heavy burden of work that faced him he enjoyed his time there. He liked his teachers and they seem to have appreciated him as a keen and intelligent pupil with a real thirst for learning.

Fig. 25 *Aerial view of the English Bridge, United Reformed Church and the Abbey. An important cluster of buildings at the end of the English Bridge: the Old Technical School, the United Reformed Church on Coleham Head, the railway viaduct, the lower end of Abbey Foregate, and Abbey Station opposite. Photographed at the end of the First World War (1918).*

There were a number of differences compared with Wilfred's previous school. Latin was not taught (which was to cause him some difficulty later), but he would learn more science in Shrewsbury than would have been available to him in Birkenhead, and Shropshire's well-known geological features were to become an attraction. Fascination with Shropshire's past developed alongside appreciation of the local landscape, and there are references to walking on Caradoc and other prominent features, and learning about the botany and distinctive geology of the region. The teachers he encountered at 'the Technical' were evidently very committed to their work and their pupils, and Wilfred saw several of them as real friends. Some of them knew his parents too, and this polite, enthusiastic and hard-working boy was evidently a real credit to their work. Harold refers several times to his brother's perpetual cleanliness, with no schoolboy grubby hands or untidy appearance.

The Owens were like most families and their friends and neighbours in pre-1914 England, with their religious faith a central part of their philosophy and daily, family life. Since Wilfred's earliest childhood, Bible study, discussion of the day's sermon and private reading of the Gospels had all been part of everyday life, and

this continued as a central thread in his approach to life throughout his years in Shrewsbury. When Wilfred was away in the school holidays, visiting friends or his cousins, or when Susan was staying with her sister for a rest, his letters frequently referred to the Sunday service, with details of services attended and including the hymns and sermon texts. In his later teens he attended the Keswick Convention, a great annual event of evangelical Christianity.

The choice of an acceptable church where the Owen family could worship and pursue their own regular Bible study was therefore an important matter, and despite Tom's Church of England attendance and background he had accepted Susan's strict Methodist upbringing and principles at the time of their marriage. Susan, however, now missed the support of Canon Robson, the clergyman in their preferred church in Birkenhead. Renowned for his preaching and his magnetic personality, he evidently had a profound influence on Wilfred, who attended Sunday School regularly in addition to family worship. In Shrewsbury, the Abbey was the obvious choice for the family: it was their parish church, Tom's family had been living in the area since the 1880s, and the marriages of both his sisters were celebrated there. Now a full resident in his own right and with his own establishment, he joined the Abbey choir and was for some time a regular sidesman there.

Throughout his school years in Birkenhead, Wilfred had enjoyed his Bible study and regular devotions, both in church and with Susan at home. So it was that these childhood years were filled with constant study of biblical language – a practice which emerged years later in his letters and poetry, from a mind filled with imagery, deep thought and ideals. Susan's principles were concerned with patience, suffering, meek acceptance of one's lot in life. One fairly short-lived development in Wilfred's inner life confirmed these instincts (and seems somewhat disconcerting to the modern mind), when he developed the practice of presenting what became known as 'Wilfred's Church'. The sitting-room table and chairs would be rearranged to represent pews and a pulpit, and Susan, skilled in embroidery, even went so far as to embroider special altar cloths, stoles and a surplice. Thus attired, Wilfred would conduct a complete evening service with a short and carefully prepared sermon. Susan supported this venture wholeheartedly, although Tom remained neutral about it and it was not long before the custom faded.

Although there is no mention of the Abbey's history and activity in Wilfred's letters, Harold has left a vivid picture of one profound and enduring pleasure in his childhood. When he and his father attended services, they would remain to hear the organist if he continued to play. The music in the fine and shadowy old church sent Harold into a trance-like state of spiritual calm and a kind of enchantment from the

Fig. 26 (left) *The young pupil-teacher. A serious gaze from Wilfred, aged about 17, conscious of the heavy burden of his studies, dividing his time between the Technical School and Wyle Cop Primary School (c.1910).*

Fig. 27 *'Mahim', no. 69 Monkmoor Road from the garden side (on the left of the image) under construction. The Owen family moved into the newly completed house in 1910.*

variations, complexity and resolution in the music. The sonorous notes of the organ, echoing round the shadowy building, evidently had a mystical effect on the child, entirely separate from any understanding of musical structure or the words attached to it. He tried to express this to his somewhat puzzled father, but his rather halting words were, in his account, brushed aside as, 'Nonsense, boy!'

In later years, the Owen children's neighbour and friend in Monkmoor Road, Mary Ragge, remembered how Tom continued to prefer the style of the Abbey services, and showed less enthusiasm when Susan came to prefer the more evangelical style of St Julian's, in Fish Street – despite the steep walk up Wyle Cop (in later years, Wilfred would push her up the hill in a wheelchair). She and Wilfred became friendly with the vicar, Norton Duncan, and his family, and it seems that Wilfred regarded it as his own church in Shrewsbury. The atmosphere there was markedly evangelical in tone, and the much more 'high church' style of St Mary's was openly criticised. Meanwhile, in search of either services or singing that were more in tune with his own instincts, Tom Owen would set off in the opposite direction to attend St Giles's church near the Column at the top of Abbey Foregate.

Fig. 28 (right) *St Julian's Church and Fish Street. St Julian's was particularly favoured by Susan Owen and Wilfred. The buildings are unchanged since that time and the scene is frequently sketched or photographed.*

Much later, in the bitter winter weather of January 1917, Wilfred and his men in the front line in France came under shell-fire during his first days in action. They were in a deep dug-out with water rising steadily around them. It was a Sunday evening, and as he stood there, trapped in the cold, wet darkness with enemy shells crashing down overhead, he thought steadily of his mother attending evensong at St Julian's at the same moment. It became one of the dreadful moments which emerged a few months later in his poem 'The Sentry', written as he recovered from incapacitating shell-shock in the spring months of that year:

> *Rain, guttering down in waterfalls of slime,*
> *Kept slush waist-high and rising hour by hour,*
> *And choked the steps too thick with clay to climb.*

Tom Owen has left little direct contribution to the family's history, but in both Wilfred's letters and Harold's memoirs his personality comes over clearly in these years. To meet, he was evidently an upright and well-built man, neatly dressed and always with well-polished shoes, with a sturdy independence and concern for his wife and four children. Harold generally felt more comfortable with his father, and somewhat resented what he saw as Susan's utter concentration on Wilfred, but nonetheless recognised his father's occasional outbursts of impatience. From his status as eldest child, and his mother's favourite, Wilfred sometimes also resented his father's 'snorts' of derision or anger, but he also developed a good relationship with him which survived some stormy adolescent conflicts.

It seems that such eruptions were caused by family arguments or by what Tom saw as idle or casual behaviour; and, although Susan's home was her domain regarding clothes, meals and attendance at school or church, Tom had his own personal domestic rules and style. He was very insistent on the importance of reading, of enjoying music and getting on well with others. He played the piano and encouraged his children to learn and, as the possessor of a strong, rich voice, he enjoyed singing. He also took delight in reading aloud to the family, relishing everyone's enjoyment of Dickens in particular, and encouraging their own independent reading. Walter Scott was another favourite, and it is possible to see echoes of Scott's language in his historical novels in some of Wilfred's early poetry. Tom and Wilfred would work together to enact dramatic scenes, and both boys relished the family style of humour. When Wilfred was away from home, both during his school years and later, his letters home often included jokes and incidents described in the universally recognised style of *Punch* magazine.

Much later Harold described a division within the family: on one hand, Susan found Wilfred a willing and responsive listener who took his daily Bible study with

Fig. 29 *Railway accident, October 1907. A major rail crash outside Shrewsbury station killed 18 people. The locomotive and tender were left lying on their sides beneath two shattered carriages, one ripped open (1907).*

her very seriously, while on the other hand Tom and Harold enjoyed more physical exercise and exploratory outdoor activities. Susan's insistence on the daily spiritual care of her children – based on her own strict Methodist childhood – as well as good manners, clean clothes and willingness to suffer setbacks patiently sharpened these differences between her two elder sons.

Tom, now in his early forties, could reasonably hope for eventual promotion to the post of Station Superintendent; but not long after their arrival he found himself at the heart of a tragic event. In October 1907 the whole community was shocked by a major crash when a night train from Manchester careered off the tight bend just outside the station. The total number of victims was 18 dead, including the engine driver and fireman, two guards, three Royal Mail workers sorting mail and eleven passengers. The three-day enquiry was attended by the future Prime Minister, David Lloyd George, then President of the Board of Trade. The funeral cortège for victims brought great crowds to watch it pass, and the graves of the three Royal Mail men and an Italian passenger can still be seen in Shrewsbury General Cemetery in Longden Road.

Fig. 30 *Funeral Cortège. The train disaster caused great distress, and the funeral of two victims, a week later, attracted large crowds to watch the procession as it passed the Abbey (18 October 1907).*

Not surprisingly, such an event had a great effect on the whole town, as well as the staff at all levels of Shrewsbury station, and Tom Owen was given the task of restoring staff morale. His approach included official occasions as well as informal encouragement, and in January 1908 he chaired a new formal evening for a large number of Joint Railways officers, a dinner with musical entertainment partly devised by Tom. Later in the year, he presided over another very positive occasion when he made a presentation to a particularly effective inspector. Both events were reported in the *Shrewsbury Chronicle*, with a note of his address at the dinner stating how happy he was to be one of their company.

At the heart of the busy railway station, Tom naturally saw more than his family of the town and the outside world, while over time it became clear that Susan was happiest when surrounded by her family at home. They clearly found the surrounding community more agreeable than their Birkenhead setting, and good friendships emerged. Shortage of money was always a challenge; modest ambition was good but must be realistic. Matters of faith, education and good manners were fundamental, along with the importance of being suitably dressed on all occasions, tidy, polite and helpful, well-spoken and respectful to others. Private lessons in piano and French should be afforded if at all possible, and at all times, it appeared, Susan's devotion to Wilfred and encouragement of his talents was constant and insistent.

As the children grew up, and with the routines of daily life manageable and regular, Susan was quite often absent on visits to her sister Emma Gunston for rest and some respite from household duties. The Gunstons' new house, 'Alpenrose', built to her husband John's own wishes and named in fond memory of holidays in Switzerland, became a happy family focus and perhaps a reminder for Susan and Emma of childhood years in Oswestry. Emma was a very committed Methodist and always strict in her attitudes and family management: on the more rare occasions when Tom Owen accompanied his family, it was clear that his favourite cigar was not to be smoked in the house, and alcohol was never allowed.

Fig. 31 *Leslie Gunston as a boy. Wilfred visited his cousins frequently and continued to exchange letters and literary efforts with Leslie throughout his life.*

Such visits were a particularly valuable consequence of Tom's employment, since he could arrange free tickets and ensure good care for his wife; and as Wilfred became old enough to travel alone, the availability of free tickets and reserved compartments provided him, in effect, with a second family. His mother, with Mary, would wave from the garden gate as he swept past in the train on his frequent visits to his aunt, uncle and congenial cousins – Gordon, Duncan, Vera and Leslie – during his school holidays.

Wilfred was a frequent and exuberant visitor in his teenage years, even launching a 'Literary and Philosophical Society' with two of his cousins and one of their local friends. They also competed in creative writing, providing evidence of Wilfred's enthusiasm and growing interest in the technicalities of writing poetry; and the household clearly formed an important element in his growing intellect – combined cheerfully with expeditions to go skating, or to see the Roman remains at local sites. His frequent letters home reflected times of high spirits, debate, skating, exploration and earnest discussion.

The Gunstons provided Wilfred with a congenial and energetic warmth and friendliness, which encouraged his sociability and literary interests. John Gunston became a serious photographer in his active retirement, and added a studio to his house. When Wilfred joined the army in 1916, his uncle was delighted to take a series of photographs of the new young officer in uniform – the only surviving visual record of his nephew as he embarked on his active service apart from a few group photographs (*see Figs. 59 & 60, pages 96 & 97*).

Wilfred also developed a good circle of friends in Shrewsbury, including the brother of one of Harold's school acquaintances, described by Harold as '... rather a serious person ...' who served in the war and later went into Holy Orders. Most of these local companions came from more prosperous families than the Owens, and attended better schools.

By 1910, Wilfred's efforts at school were prominent in letters to his mother, who was again on a visit to her sister Emma Gunston. Now in the first year of his formal pupil-teacher training, in the spring he strove to come first in exams. The news was mixed:

> *F. Watson remains impregnable! For all my exam successes (e.g. French 91, History 94) her army of Term Marks she has so diligently mustered are superior to mine. I am still 2nd therefore ... We are all wasting a tremendous lot of time ... I did one exercise no less than 5 times before it secured satisfaction! We (boys) are all working away in Recreation Time in the Gay Meadow* [the public recreation ground by the Severn, soon to be the town's football ground], *mowing and rolling 2 Tennis Courts. I hope to play soon, may I? Already I have had some Cricket there. Hockey & Football go on at the same time!*

A year later, in May 1911, Wilfred was again writing to Susan about aspects at school which reveal his enthusiasms:

> *... on Saturday we, the 'Botany People' ... started by train for Condover* [five miles south of Shrewsbury] *for the expedition to Lyth Hill. ... Miss Wright's sister was one of the party. She knows no Botany but has a passionate love of English literature, with the result that when we found each other out we spent the rest of the day comparing opinions, agreeing and disagreeing, quoting and counter-quoting, somewhat to the dismay of the other members of the party who (possibly) did not know what the subject of our rapt conversation was ...*

A very different kind of activity was significant for both Tom and Wilfred, when father and son travelled together twice for short holidays in France. Wilfred soon discovered that his efforts to learn French at school had been effective, and he enjoyed the experience of engaging in conversation with anyone ready to talk to him. On the boat to Brittany in 1908 and 1909 he chatted and explored happily and freely, unknowingly laying the foundations for the much deeper knowledge of the country, the language and the people that lay ahead.

Although the river defined many aspects of town life, and was a great resource for the young family's leisure, there is very little direct mention of Shrewsbury itself in either Harold's memoirs or Wilfred's letters – apart from Harold's dislike of the schools he attended. The only aspect of the centre that held interest for Wilfred – and this can be seen in his letters and various poetic references – was the town museum. The fine stone buildings near the station and castle had been the home of Shrewsbury School since its foundation in 1552, but in the 1880s it had moved out of the picturesque and historic (but undoubtedly cramped) premises to larger accommodation across the river.

The old town buildings, complete with a fine statue of Darwin outside, were taken over and used for the borough's free museum and public library. Wilfred explored its

Fig. 32 *Unveiling the statue of Charles Darwin. The controversial scientist was educated at Shrewsbury School. General disapproval of his ideas caused concern and security worries on this occasion (1897).*

contents frequently and began to understand more about local history, particularly the Roman presence near Shrewsbury over several centuries. Echoes of his intense interest in the distant past emerged in the earliest poems of his more mature years. Rome and the Romans appear many times over, with the sense of the ancient rulers and indigenous British communities with their life in the woods and hillsides.

His one known poem relating to the town refers to this interest in the classical past, in the form of a short verse of uncertain date (*see Appendix 2, page 127*). It may have been written in the spring of 1914 as part of a joint exercise of the kind he shared with his cousins – or, possibly, according to another editor, in May 1917, when he was recovering from the first effects of shell-shock. It is a 'roundel', an old form of verse, and refers to the only statue in the Quarry park, a large lead figure of Hercules. In 1851 this classical eighteenth-century copy of a famous nude Roman figure stood by the main gates into the Quarry, opposite St Chad's Church. To avoid offence, it was placed with its back to the town, but this was still not quite satisfactory and in 1881 it was moved to the present-day more discreet site by the river-edge.

The roundel contains some of the mock-medieval language that Wilfred liked to affect in his school years, and the theme is Hercules' weariness in the face of local bye-laws and sleepy people. Otherwise, Wilfred's letters to his mother occasionally refer to neighbours or, somewhat dismissively, to the girls who came in to look after the house in Susan's absence, in reference to domestic arrangements in their particular part of town.

As so often, the everyday home-town background went unnoticed as the routine basis for the elements of personal life. Independent adult life, earning one's living, was something important but undefinable for the teenage Wilfred Owen, to be worried about – especially with parents or teachers – but separate and remote from his constant reading. In the spring of 1911, he wrote to his mother about his future and, like so many adolescents before and since, despaired of ever finding an occupation that was both attractive and attainable:

> *Really, indecision is rapidly turning into distraction. When I begin to eliminate from my list all those professions which are impossible (seemingly) from a financial point of view, and then those which I feel disinclined for – it leaves nothing. But is my inclination to matter after all? ... If it must be done, I suppose I am not too young to destroy all my love of literature and such study, and turn to Office Routine, Customs, Revenues, Taxation, etc. – (I suppose this is what is meant by Civil Service, but as a matter of fact my ideas of this life are of the vaguest) ...*

3 SPREADING HORIZONS

blessed with gold

IN 1911, the local newspaper carried disturbing news of difficult labour relations, the Irish question, demonstrators being shot by troops, talk of famine and revolution overseas. There was a national rail strike – although no mention of it appears in relation to Tom Owen and Shrewsbury station. However, in Shrewsbury the Flower Show went ahead as usual, and the newly crowned King George V was honoured with a mood of celebration, balloon rides, the amazing sight of aircraft overhead, and lavish fireworks. Domestic matters in Shrewsbury seemed generally undisturbed, and after four years in the town the ordinary incidents, sights and people of Shrewsbury had become part of the Owen family's daily activities. Domestic security and routine were creating habit and the memories that would follow the children into adulthood, marking the lives of both Wilfred in his letters and poems, and Harold in his memoirs.

One major event in the life of the Owen family had been the decision in 1910 to move into a larger house, with a good garden and more space for the four adolescent children. It was only a few minutes' walk away from Cleveland Place, up the street and round the corner into Monkmoor Road where (as with Tom and Susan's first household in Shrewsbury in 1897) they became the first tenants in a new house. Then they

Fig. 33 *'Mahim', Monkmoor Road. The Owen family moved here in 1907. The house remains clearly recognisable apart from the low front wall, which no longer exists. Wilfred occupied the top attic room.*

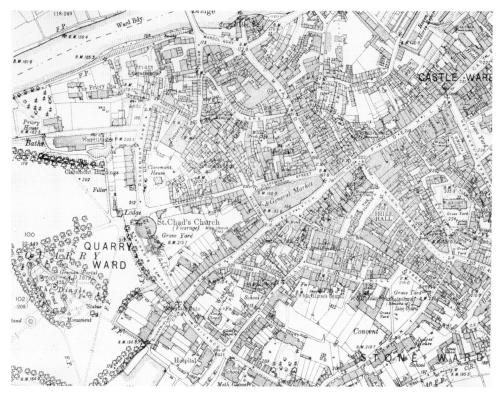

Fig. 34 *Street map of Shrewsbury from the late 1800s or the early twentieth century, showing the tight street pattern of the town centre, including part of the Quarry with the Dingle and the Baths.*

had invoked Susan's childhood home with its name, but this time the new establishment, officially numbered 68, was to be called 'Mahim' at Tom's insistence. He would never explain the background, but it apparently held happy memories of his years in India in the 1880s, before his marriage. As before, Wilfred took over the attic bedroom, with a table squeezed in under the dormer window. Chilly but secluded, it was the ideal retreat for a boy of 17 to spend the long hours of school work, reading and applying his mind to his early literary efforts. It also had a fine, open view – over the rough grass terrain of the old racecourse across the road, with fields, the river and the steep slope of Haughmond Hill beyond.

Shrewsbury's one-time racecourse had occupied a large stretch of the open ground spreading out from Monkmoor Road towards the river. After considerable success in the mid-nineteenth century it had failed as a business, and the area was now used for rough grazing, agricultural shows and fairs. Harold recounts a somewhat different use of the ground, when he and Wilfred would catch the ponies which grazed there and ride around on them. From their new house in Monkmoor Road this sense of expansive leisure waiting almost at their door for them was an open invitation for the two brothers to explore. The old grandstand buildings were still in place, and in the summer of 1914 the site was graced by a royal visit, when King George V interrupted the preoccupations of that fateful year to attend the Royal Agricultural Show.

How well did the family know the town itself as a whole? As well as households of every kind and size, it was a world of workshops and trades, and general stores with plentiful sales staff keen to show off an astonishing range of goods. As might be expected, Wilfred's letters make no reference to shopping; but such areas as Frankwell, the Welsh Bridge, or the town streets beyond the station are also absent. The demands of good manners, occasional errands and his mother's local friendships ensured that their own area was the comfortable and unremarkable background to everyday life, and Wilfred made friends with the sons of local families. Within the town, he naturally knew the station – Tom's domain and the point of departure for the family's frequent rail trips – while the museum became a regular destination.

Apart from Tom's close involvement with the Shrewsbury railway staff after the accident in 1907, and the constant to and fro of people through the station, we know little about public events or daily life outside the family. In Birkenhead, beyond the demands of his employment at the busy Woodside railway terminus, Tom had been drawn to the bustle and energy of the docks, the shipping, and the mixture of nationalities which reminded him of his one big adventure, working for an Indian railway company many years earlier. His enthusiasm for the sea and everything to do with shipping, and the experience of working his way out to India in his bachelor days, once led him to invite some Indian sailors to their house in Birkenhead. The children were delighted and intrigued to see these polite brown-skinned men, in their own style of clothes, who arrived bearing gifts for everyone and communicated with little English but much goodwill on both sides. It was an enjoyable occasion for Tom, but Susan was somewhat less convinced.

One of their Shrewsbury neighbours later commented that Susan was truly happiest in her own home and organising the family. Mary Ragge, who enjoyed the company of the young Owens and loved Susan dearly, remembered her later years as always open-hearted and welcoming, a 'very sweet' person with a light and gentle voice. Mary Owen was also much loved by her family and their friends, but from childhood onwards her life was devoted to helping her mother to run the house. One of the consequences of the war ahead would be the number of girls of her generation whose potential husbands were lost in the cataclysm, but Mary's physical frailty and commitment to the family household also seem to have hindered ideas of independence or marriage.

For both Harold and Wilfred, the difference between opportunities beyond 'the Technical' and those available to boys who attended one of the major fee-paying schools became increasingly clear. In this respect, as in many others, the war years led to many unexpected friendships and overcame many such social divisions. Early in 1918, when Wilfred was in Scarborough, back on light duties with the Army after recovering from shell-shock, he found particular pleasure in a cheerful and warm friendship with one of his fellow-officers who taught Classics at Shrewsbury School.

The river provided endless diversion and leisure activity for town-dwellers, with two rowing clubs, and plenty of boats for hire, since regattas, river excursions and boating picnics were a large part of social life for many young people. Participation often indicated a certain degree of wealth and social style, and in Susan's eyes represented a way of life that contradicted her faith and which, in any case, her family could not afford. Other patterns of simple leisure along the river were a regular element of family life, particularly for Tom. As early as 1908 Wilfred wrote to his mother, who was away visiting the Gunstons, that he and his father had taken a picnic on the river and shared the rowing to outlying areas near home. Tom always delighted in being out of doors, taking the children out to explore hedgerows, fields and the river bank in the early mornings. Harold seems to have enjoyed these early morning outings more than Wilfred, but both boys learned how to observe wildlife. Their neighbouring young friends, Mary and John Ragge, joined the two boys as they roamed and explored, and it was clearly understood that although birds' nests were a delight to observe, eggs must never be taken.

The Owens knew of several places where swimming was easy to manage – complete with bushes for modesty's sake, for no one must see any of them actually changing or drying themselves. Such expeditions were mostly for the boys, with the scale of their explorations growing as they grew. However, Mary Ragge records a moment when three or four of the children from the two families were enjoying the river bank and she began to peel off her stockings in order to paddle at the edge of the water. Colin, the youngest of the party, whispered doubtfully to one of his brothers that he did not think she should do this – clearly Susan's ideas on modesty and decency, and her firm instructions to her children, were under threat. As they all grew older they explored further afield, and Harold describes the many pleasures of being at liberty along the dusty lanes and in the fields.

One place outside the town took on a shared significance for the family. The small village of Uffington lay across the river from the end of Monkmoor Road, where the ferryman could be summoned with shouts to take them across in his rope-hauled craft. The two boys would explore Haughmond Abbey ruins and the hill, and on fine Sundays the family came together for Evensong at Uffington Church, with Susan being pushed along in her wheelchair. As well as the services there, they all enjoyed the quiet walk

Fig. 35 (right) *The staff of Singleton & Cole, tobacco manufacturers, cigarette and cigar makers. Tom Owen was an intermittent but keen smoker. The company premises in Mardol have an intricately carved doorway, with the figure above promoting the delights of pipe-smoking (c.1900).*

Fig. 36 *Castlefields footbridge, which replaced the old Underdale–Castle Walk ferry, used by Tom Owen (1916).*

home on summer evenings through the water-meadows and wild flowers, with swallows darting overhead.

Harold in particular loved Uffington, and would go there on his own to paint, to explore and talk to the villagers. At first Harold went with Wilfred, and later alone or with Colin, his pocket-money pennies saved to pay for the ferry. Ten years later, moments and memories of Shropshire beauty in this quiet place emerged in Wilfred's writing, in the poetry that grew from his experience of war. In April 1917, ten years after the move to Shrewsbury, he was in the front line with his troops near the French city of Saint Quentin, preparing to attack an enemy outpost. As he led his men up a quiet hillside, hidden from their opponents and the onslaught that awaited them over the hill-top, they paused to rest. His poem 'Spring Offensive' refers to this moment of peace, intensified by an awareness of the acute danger ahead. There was calm sunshine, brambles clinging to them, and they could see that, '… buttercups had blessed with gold their slow boots coming up'.

Much later, in 1931, Harold made a margin note in Edmund Blunden's edition of his brother's poems, recording his pleasure of looking with 'delighted wonder' at their 'shoes and stockings flushed with gold'. Another twenty years later still, Harold's memoirs revived the memory once more: referring to the poem 'Spring Offensive', he recorded this link between the summer meadows and the terrible situation on a French battlefield as a deliberate echo by his brother.

Fig. 37 *Uffington ferry, frequently used by the Owens.*

In her old age Mary Ragge remembered with much amusement a very different incident on the path to Uffington: on one occasion a substantial cow had settled herself comfortably and immovably against the stile which lay between the families and the ferry. This was funny for the children, but caused consternation among the three ladies present – Susan Owen, Mrs Ragge and her sister – until, fortunately, a diversion was discovered which enabled them all to continue.

Wilfred was well aware that despite his literary ambitions he did not have a brilliant mind and needed intense hard work to expand his knowledge. It is not difficult to imagine him hurrying along the road past Shrewsbury Abbey, the classic young

Fig. 38 *Cottages at Uffington. All of the Owens enjoyed visiting Uffington, crossing the river by ferry to attend Evening Service in the village church (early twentieth century).*

student figure bowed under the weight of his books and the need to read, to learn, to expand his mind and knowledge and to do well at school. No time to be wasted. On the whole he was successful, enjoying the ideas and individuals that he encountered at school, and taking pleasure in reciting and acting. Preparing essays and learning how to read attentively, to use the English language and write effectively, were all part of his central ambition.

Two teachers, Miss Wright and Miss Jones, were his favourites, and indeed became family friends. It is probably these two young women who should be recognised for fostering his wider interests – geology, botany and biology – as well as intensive study of the English classics. His early request for a geologist's hammer helped him to explore Shropshire's rich geological past, and this practical understanding of the landscape enabled Wilfred to make essential links between the land and poets such as Wordsworth, Keats and Shelley. Recitation and acting were a pleasure too: useful talents for anyone aspiring to be a teacher – or a poet. He aimed to achieve top marks in all exams, and was deeply disappointed by those of his fellow-pupils – girls as well as boys – who sometimes beat him to top place.

For the two school years from September 1909 until July 1911, Wilfred was a part-time pupil-teacher at Wyle Cop School, just above The Lion Hotel, where only part of

Fig. 39 *Uffington Canal, with its bridge and Haughmond Hill in the background, was another favoured place for walking. Harold in particular loved exploring and painting here, alone or with his brothers.*

the school's buildings survives (in private ownership) on the edge of a large car park. Although The Lion makes no appearance in Harold's memoirs, it was a considerable landmark in the town, and both Disraeli and Dickens were among its famous visitors. Wilfred's practical teaching meant dividing his time equally between his regular matriculation classes at The Technical and instilling basic education into children in the primary school. The only surviving element of this particular elementary school (the kitchens building) lies in what is now a calm and pleasant area close to the immediate centre of the town. However, in the early 1900s the school catered for children from some very poor and overcrowded areas. Harold was a pupil there for his final years of junior schooling, and speaks of it with disdain for his fellow-pupils. Although the brothers probably overlapped at the school, Harold's memoirs make no mention of his older brother being a pupil-teacher while he himself was one of the pupils.

Although Wilfred rarely mentioned school companions in the letters of his schoolboy years, he was delighted to meet some of them during his war service; one of the inevitable coincidences in the vast army of men constantly on the move. It was typical of the whole complexity of the war that a familiar face would suddenly appear in a crowd of otherwise anonymous soldiers. In May 1917, as Wilfred arrived at a Casualty

Clearing Station at Gailly, on the Somme, he found himself face to face with 'Fred Hartop of the Technical', as he put it in his next letter home, referring to him as one of the 'Good Old Sort'. Hartop, who held the undemanding role of Pack Store Corporal in the army medical corps, welcomed him with enthusiasm, talked happily of their school-days and lent him books to pass the time: it must have been very reassuring to find the flavour of life in Shrewsbury reappearing in the midst of warfare.

One of their local friends commented in later life that he considered that Wilfred appeared too snobbish to feel sympathy for children who suffered from social deprivation – but in his younger years Wilfred had often been required to take responsibility for his younger siblings at home, or take them for walks when his mother was unable to do so. This experience of taking charge, instructing and managing while still a child must also have been valuable after he left home, when gaining independence as a teacher in France and then as a junior officer in the First World War. At this time, however, his main challenge was the burden of school work, with two demanding headmasters to satisfy – Mr Timpany at the pupil-teacher centre, and Mr Lightbown at the Cop school.

Amidst the pressures in his later teenage years, Wilfred quite often complained

Fig. 40 *Pengwern Boat Club. A group sitting on the river bank and a man and woman in their boat on the river. This was not the Owens' style of leisure activity (c.1910)*

– like so many adolescents – that his home town was boring. On his own he joined the YMCA and went out cycling with other members, and knew boys in several local families who were more prosperous than the Owens and attended better schools. These included Stanley Webb, one of a large family in Abbey Foregate, who enjoyed cycling out with Wilfred to the great Roman site of Uriconium, near Wroxeter. Here they could enjoy digging around the site, dreaming of ancient Rome and the great civilisation which had left so many tantalising remains. The site was, as it still is, remarkable for the impressive remains of a large wall that defines the heart of the former city.

The silent evidence of the long Roman presence in Shropshire fascinated and enlarged Wilfred's mental horizons, and clearly encouraged his imagination in relation to the distant past. Ploughing and fence-building constantly threw up pottery and stonework, so that local farmhouses and fields held – and no doubt still hold – local finds, or stone used for building. The city lay on the track of Watling Street, an important link with the rest of the country, established by the Romans and almost certainly following even older local tracks. Uriconium was an important site on the Roman network of communication and sound roads, and the site was close to the River Severn, with shallows to cross over, or for river trade. Wilfred's imagination and searching was stimulated by the Roman remains in the borough museum, housed in what had been the premises of Shrewsbury School – and therefore Charles Darwin's schoolroom.

This was another strong local link to the past: although Charles Darwin is not mentioned in Wilfred's letters or in Harold's memoirs, his ideas were inescapable.

Fig. 41 *Kingsland Bridge and 'Boats for Hire' seen from the Quarry. The boat-houses of Shrewsbury School and the Pengwern Boat Club lie beyond the bridge, on the left (c.1910).*

Fig. 42 *Wyle Cop School. Two women teachers with 14 girls and 18 boys outside the school, next to the Lion Hotel, where Wilfred Owen undertook his teaching practice (1911).*

Darwin was born and educated in Shrewsbury, and the breadth of his evolutionary thinking was viewed with whole-hearted distrust in the town, where such revolutionary scientific studies and theories made him wholly unacceptable in conventional circles. The irony of inspecting Roman remains in Darwin's former schoolroom must have occurred to Wilfred, who was already fascinated by geology and history; and perhaps Darwin's understanding of the aeons of geological development can be seen in Owen's poem 'Miners'. This was his first poem to appear in a national publication, and the first one for which he was paid, in 1918; a poem linking the work of miners in England with his wartime experience of their labour in the front line.

On a later visit with Stanley Webb, Wilfred watched a team of archaeologists on a major dig to uncover and identify the foundations and remains of Uriconium, which today lie largely under protective turf. The boys wondered again about the civilisation that had created the mosaic pavement and the great inscribed tablet which once welcomed citizens into the Forum, with its exceptionally fine carving that set the standard for elegant lettering. The mosaics were uncovered, examined and measured before being covered up again for their preservation; while a ditch beside the Roman street produced a quantity of fine, red pottery in prime condition – now a prized exhibit in the town museum.

Fig. 43 *Uriconium Roman site, within easy bicycling distance of Shrewsbury, to visit and explore for Roman remains (a nineteenth-century view).*

On this occasion in 1912, when he was struggling to sustain his ambitions from Dunsden vicarage, he was stung by the sight of these archaeological specialists. Their careful searching reminded him sharply of his desperate wish for a university degree in order to pursue his own further career. He left the site, grumbling and resentful of their knowledge, and the glimpse they had offered, unknowingly, of the sort of life he longed for. Wilfred's early education in Birkenhead had included some Latin, which he was unable to pursue at Shrewsbury Technical School. Unlike the fellow-officers he would encounter in the undreamed-of war years to come, he lacked a real grounding in classical literature. His knowledge came from well-known myths of the ancient age and from English writers who held the classical past in high regard for their creativity and mastery of the arts. It was enough to create an imagined world of Roman people and life, which deepened his sense of place in the Shropshire countryside and later emerged in his poetry.

This fascination with the Roman remains and the ancient legends and myths of the classical world combined to become the source for one of his strongest early poems. 'Uriconium' was written in 1913, and although it reflects the limitations of schoolboy language and the influence of Victorian poetry, it is a revealing and sustained long poem. Roman heroic figures, their deeds and beliefs, their underworld and the remnants of their life so close to his own home, all strengthened his view of antiquity. No doubt this familiarity with the Roman site so near home encouraged his imagination

Fig. 44 *Shrewsbury Borough Library and Museum, originally Shrewsbury School, in Castle Gates. Wilfred's imagination was stirred by the museum's collection of Roman remains from Uriconium, which inspired his poetic ideas (1891).*

and poetry, including the widely-known classical Latin expression of heroic patriotism, 'Dulce et decorum est pro patria mori': it is sweet and fitting to die for one's country.

Great names in English literature provided the basis for a growing identification with nineteenth-century poets and, for a boy born in 1893, figures such as Wordsworth and Tennyson felt very close as representative models for Wilfred's concept of expressive English. Tom Owen encouraged all his children to read regularly, but nothing that might be seen as 'modern' or 'avant-garde' would appear in the household, and school provided a very traditional culture. Although Tom took pleasure in reading aloud to his family, there were no opportunities to meet or talk with writers or academic scholars. Wilfred's models became the young Romantic poets – Shelley supremely and then Keats; and their ideals and frustrations perhaps added to their attraction for an adolescent with his own immense ambitions for literary skill and comprehension. Such leanings were Wilfred's own personal enthusiasm, but music was a shared family diversion at home, as Tom's pleasure in singing and listening to the church choir or organ extended to playing the piano and accompanying his own singing – and, as Wilfred grew older, the two of them would tussle over access to the piano.

Over time, the warmth of friendship between Wilfred and Harold grew with recognition of each other's qualities; but the differences continued to be striking. Wilfred's opinions and feelings about people and activities can be discerned through his letters and comments about Harold and his character. Also, of course, as he grew to maturity, we can see his urgent and imaginative search for ways to express his inner thoughts and to share the expression of others' feelings. As he found his true voice in the war years, his young, self-imposed apprenticeship in the craft of writing enabled him to express the fierce realities of war, through his friendships, observations and enthusiasms.

Harold's memoirs show a constant search for reality. The general impression – conveying a very real sense of grievance in later life – is of an energetic boy frustrated by his own circumstances and family life but keen to observe, to draw and to paint the scene around him. In 1911 he was a student at the Art School, in the same premises as Wilfred's Pupil-Teacher Centre, and taking great interest in the art of stencilling. He undertook a commission from Wilfred to create a book-cover, based on a design sent to him with careful indications of style and general colouring. In another striking insight, his memoirs, written in comfortable circumstances, show his imagination and sensitive younger self which found expression in several almost hallucinatory or mystical experiences.

In the spring of 1911 Wilfred took the final exams at the Technical School, which would qualify him to be employed as an Uncertificated Teacher. Success here did not seem in question, but it offered a profession without any chance of promotion, even within the elementary school system. With his head teachers' warnings ringing in his ears, he became determined to sit the London University Matriculation examination as the starting point for its external university degree course. His efforts at the Shrewsbury Pupil-Teacher Centre were rewarded with distinctions in both English and French (the only local candidate to achieve this), and although the Matriculation examination would be a further challenge, a good pass would set him on the path towards the degree course that he hoped for most dearly. The awkward question of sufficient funding remained alarmingly uncertain, but in the few months between the Pupil-Teacher Centre examination in April and the Matriculation examination in September in London, he enrolled on a postal course to prepare himself independently.

By that summer, Wilfred realised that he was not cut out for elementary teaching – particularly in circumstances which would tie him down to its most basic form for the rest of his working life – and sought advice from various people. Mrs Timpany, wife of his head teacher at The Technical, repeated her warnings about the nature of the teaching for which he would be qualified, and the iniquities of the education system at that time; and in June, on a brief holiday to the Gunston family, Wilfred sought advice from their local vicar. He advised the earnest youth to seek a loan from a rich relation in order to undertake a full-time university degree course (not a practical possibility in Wilfred's case). Alternatively, in the absence of financial support, a pass at matriculation would qualify him to undertake an external degree while earning his living, perhaps as a teacher (although the workload would be almost impossibly demanding).

There was another possibility: to find a position as an assistant to a Church of England parson who could provide board and lodging with a small allowance – valuable part-time employment, useful experience in the parish and sufficient time to work for the external degree course. It would enable Wilfred to live and work in a supportive intellectual atmosphere, perhaps with some coaching for the academic course. Susan in particular found this appealing. She had long hoped that her eldest and dearest son would go into the church himself, and felt that in the long term a post of this kind could lead him towards ordination.

Very fortunately, a suitable opening emerged at this point, conveniently close to Kidmore End and the Gunstons, in the household of the Reverend Herbert Wigan, the evangelically-minded vicar of the rural village of Dunsden, near Reading. Revd Wigan already had one assistant but sought another, and Wilfred – as the nephew of Emma Gunston, with a sound grasp of doctrine and scripture, able to play the piano and an experienced elementary teacher – was immediately seen as a very useful addition to the parish. In the meantime the self-imposed course of study by correspondence included sample essay questions and reading lists; and for Wilfred, now aged 18, the work it entailed became part of his maturing adult awareness and thought.

The Matriculation exam in September 1911 required Wilfred's presence in London over three days. He was one of around 600 candidates (including many from overseas), and although some papers enabled him to show his knowledge of favourite writers, it was generally agreed that it was a particularly difficult set of papers. Afterwards, he stayed on for several more days to explore the capital, with visits to Hampton Court and Kew, and twice to the theatre. Keats drew him on a series of pilgrimages – to the British Museum, the National Portrait Gallery and Hampstead.

In October he heard that he had passed the exam – an achievement to be proud of since he was one of very few who had been successful on the basis of private study. It counted as the initial exam for the London University external degree, and so he was now technically an undergraduate with a defined course of study ahead. He bought the cap and gown to which he was entitled, enjoyed wearing them whenever possible, and moved into residence in Dunsden vicarage.

Wilfred's eighteen months at Dunsden became a period of intense development towards maturity, a path littered with valuable experience and insights into other people's lives and beliefs – and, ultimately, the realisation that he was on the wrong track. This stage of moving from home and school into the adult world was an obvious challenge in this somewhat isolated rural parish, and he learned a great deal in ways that he could not realise at the time. Many of his experiences at Dunsden he clearly enjoyed; some, however, he did not. Wilfred found out the hard way, for example, that Dunsden church's great Excursion for village children could be a real trial, as he wrote home in July 1912:

> *I rose (bitterly regretting I had ever promised to join such a detestable Excursion) at three o'clock; had breakfast by semi-candlelight … and entered the compartment labelled 'Dunsden' – which might as well have been ticketed Demonsden or my compartment in Purgatory itself.*
>
> *Such a flesh-tortured three hours did I spend in it. The Vicar perhaps had the worst time of it going – pins stuck into all his limbs – paper missiles flicked at him from teeth-holden catapults – his hat snatched away – his paper bashed about – and so on. It is only fair to state, however, that now and again he would grasp an urchin, and thwack, lam, hide, beat, belabour, whack, smack, flog, flail, thump, lick, and kick the creature till the tears swam round its eyes. Coming home, I was the sufferer; for I kept slipping into Lethe, and being pulled out again by the frantic behaviour of one boy – who, being quick-witted and fond of leading, managed to make everybody laugh at him … The Vicar sat like a log through it all; and seemed to see, feel, hear and think of – nothing. Not even did he show the least sign of perturbation when the Arch-imp shrieked 'Here comes Satan! Here's the devil!' on seeing his own reflection on the Carriage-Window.*

By the early days of 1913, he knew that he had come to the end of what Dunsden could offer him. Seen from Shrewsbury, it had appeared as a position to be proud of and a good basis for his cherished future prospects. It also provided accommodation, occupation and time to study in an atmosphere of strong religious belief with a well-educated mentor, and without the distractions of urban life. Back at Mahim in Monkmoor Road, Wilfred's departure for an indefinite period had changed the pattern of domestic life, and the absence of the eldest son must have affected the whole family. Susan and Tom still had three children at home to sustain the liveliness and chatter, requiring constant meals and clean clothes, but Susan must have missed her eldest son's presence deeply.

It is frustrating not to know what she wrote to her cherished eldest son, but his letters to her make interesting reading. We can suppose that the contents were read, or made known, to the whole family, for it was standard practice for mothers to send and receive family news and keep in touch. Communication with his mother in particular was always essential to Wilfred's wellbeing. He knew that she would share his news with his father, and his siblings also received informative letters. Letter-writing was recognised as an art, and Wilfred's letters to Susan were vivid, informative, often entertaining but always written with considerable thought and eloquence. He wrote freely about his activities, and what he saw of rural poverty and deprivation. He found the fate of the old people particularly shocking, as he wrote to his sister Mary, a few weeks after arrival:

> *Numbers of the old people cannot read; those who can seldom do so. Scores of them have passed their whole lives in the same stone box with a straw lid, which they call their cottage; and are numbed to all interests beyond it.*

Not all of them had faith in a glorious afterlife to support them.

Traces of the popular young Mr Owen's activities can also be found in multiple records of Dunsden life; in the notes of parish meetings, Sunday School, administrative papers, the boys' club and church archives. Despite the early attractions of the village as a good solution to Wilfred's difficulties, it did not offer an easy transition from a very protective home atmosphere to the adult independence and responsibility that was required. Wilfred knew by now the limits of what he could discuss with his mother – such as his current reading and his state of health – but his anxieties and minute details of minor ailments described in letters from Dunsden often seem to indicate a state of depression or anxiety. Susan's own strong and unquestioning evangelical commitment made it impossible for him to raise questions of faith and, as Harold emphasised, unpleasant matters or a 'difficult' topic (such as sex or any question of genuine religious faith) were simply not discussed. Good manners and appearance, and attention to one's elders, were the first consideration, and Susan's own reading interests did not extend to cover all the ideas and instincts which fascinated Wilfred.

In an urban setting, a period of practical employment combined with study would have enabled Wilfred to recognise more clearly the complexity of adult life, and perhaps find a balance between his religious belief, the facts of ordinary working lives and the ideas he encountered in his favourite authors. His chosen reading still concentrated on nineteenth-century writers, covering the idealism and imagination of Shelley and Keats, and the descriptions of human nature and poverty-stricken lives in the novels of Dickens. As he grew to adulthood and read ever more widely he realised more fully the truths of life and belief which fed his growing and profound discomfort over social deprivation and poverty.

It seemed unreasonable – although it was entirely normal for the time – that the Revd Herbert Wigan, as a representative of the more prosperous ruling classes and a key figure in village life, should live in warmth and comfort, while his young assistant was dealing daily with the poverty-stricken rural poor. The vicar's comfortable life and

Fig. 45 *Dunsden Vicarage. The large, comfortable house and garden, staffed to take care of all daily needs, where Wilfred spent nearly two years in his first independent experience away from home (1911–13).*

insistence on a local campaign for religious revival in his parish provided an awkward contrast with Wilfred's growing experience and philosophy. It was unfortunate that, although the vicar was a genial person in everyday life, he regarded poetry as a distraction from the sources of true enlightenment; and although Revd Wigan's own attitudes had shifted markedly from strong High Church sympathies in his early days to an equally strong commitment to the simplicity of evangelical thought and practice, he was not an easy conversationalist. Like many people of his age, Wilfred found himself isolated in internal debates and difficulties over matters of faith, life and death.

He could reflect, perhaps, on the contrast with Shrewsbury, which certainly contained poverty and miserable housing, but did at least provide wider employment than Dunsden, and diversity without the complexity and dangers of heavily industrialised cities. Difficulties began to emerge. The summer of 1912 defined the conflict in his life between success in Dunsden, his additional responsibilities together with his growing antipathy to Revd Wigan's forcefully expressed pattern of faith, and his continuing determination to work for a university degree course.

The first significant event was a holiday in the household of Nellie Bulman, Susan's childhood governess. Now a prosperous widow, she lived near Kelso in the

Scottish Borders with her adult daughter Blanche and two sons, and they were all determined to give 'Susie' and her family a really good holiday. There was fishing and golf, time to read quietly, and lively company. Wilfred was reserved and aware of the social differences between his family and the more prosperous Bulmans; but Harold, now fourteen and a student at the Art School, enjoyed himself tremendously. The young Bulmans, together with Blanche's fiancé Walter Forrest, were cheerful and energetic and enjoyed introducing their friends and taking the young Owens fishing or shooting. There was an expedition to Edinburgh for Wilfred, to show him the city, and he was also able to visit Walter Scott's house, Abbotsford, and the battlefield of Flodden. Blanche's father had died some years earlier, but his business continued until the 1950s, with Blanche as a director, working with the landed gentry on their estates and managing their large houses.

Interestingly, it appears that there was another direct link between Shrewsbury and the Bulmans of Kelso: Shrewsbury School records a former pupil from the town, Lieutenant Andrew Bulman of the King's Own Scottish Borderers. He left the school in 1907, studied architecture and was part of the same company as Nellie Bulman's late husband. As an officer in the Territorial Force he was posted to Gallipoli in 1915, and was killed there.

This welcome time with his family was followed by the Keswick Convention, an Anglican gathering in the Lake District in late July (also attended by his cousins Dorothy and Vera Gunston), which assembled a large number of clerics and many hundreds of enthusiastic supporters. Camp conditions were spartan but at the prayer meetings Wilfred was deeply impressed by a group of young miners and the strength of their commitment to their faith. At the time he was teaching himself physics and learning about mining in his correspondence course, having already enjoyed learning geology at school. Back home, Wilfred could enjoy further time to talk and debate with his mother about his present and future, although his visit to Uriconium and the archaeological site with Stanley Webb at this time was an unhappy reminder of how far he was from achieving his intellectual goals.

October in Dunsden brought another significant occasion in Wilfred's developing mind when he attended a funeral for the first time in his life – the outcome of a shocking accident in which a local mother and her young daughter were killed. They were riding on a cartload of household belongings as they moved to another village, when the horses bolted and the cart was violently overturned. This intensely moving double funeral affected him deeply and resulted in one of the earliest of his mature poems, 'Deep Under Turfy Grass'. It hints at his doubts about the concept of life after death and how human life and belief can confront such personal tragedies.

Fig. 46 (right) *Wilfred in the garden at Dunsden Vicarage, now 19 years of age. In his first venture after leaving school he was working as assistant to the vicar (1911).*

Fig. 47 *Colin, Wilfred, Susan and Harold, with May and Tom in front, taken in the Kelso garden of Nellie Bulman, an old and trusted friend from Oswestry. Their clothes reflect the style of the day and the children's ages, particularly Colin's Norfolk jacket and knickerbocker trousers (1912).*

Wilfred's letters give characteristic, mock-humorous descriptions which either dramatise or make light of various incidents in his Dunsden life (a fall from his bike, a dizzy fit in the house), but he was evidently in an unhappy state of mind, and his parents visited him several times to reassure both their son and themselves. By mid-December he was writing home about his nerves, unpleasant symptoms of depression and anxiety, and the sense of an impending storm over 'theological distractions' – a reference to his growing distaste for outspoken declarations of faith in personal suffering and redemption through faith. By this time he was seriously unhappy about the conventions in which he had been so carefully instructed.

The first letter to Susan after his return to Dunsden after Christmas refers to the solemn and stiff atmosphere in the Vicarage, and a confrontation and breakdown in his relationship with the community was inevitable. The final test came in January 1913, when he wrote home about a 'furore' in the Vicarage – and unfortunately a potentially highly revealing portion of a letter from this time is missing which might have provided more details. Wilfred was in a state of nervous tension and depression, and great unhappiness over an active revivalist campaign in the village. A further complication and reason for misgivings was Wilfred's particular friendship and interest in one of the more intelligent and intellectually enquiring boys in the parish, Vivien Rampton. The discovery that a series of private conversations and piano lessons had been taking place in the Vicarage, but without the vicar's knowledge, caused a considerable uproar. Revd Wigan must have been distressed to find his confidence so misplaced, but after some further uncomfortable interviews Wilfred made his feelings clear: that he could not reconcile his views of Christianity with what he knew of science and literature. Susan visited the Vicarage, but evidently without any success in resolving the impasse, and in mid-February 1913 Wilfred packed his possessions and left Dunsden.

Rather than spending another year before taking the next of his London University external degree exams, Wilfred took the advice of Edith Morley, Professor of English at Reading University College. She had taken a very positive interest in this keen young student who lacked guidance and she now urged Wilfred to sit for a scholarship to the College in 1913, which was designed to benefit the candidate of 'most promise' and would enable him to study full-time as he longed to do.

He was depressed and in an alarming state of ill-health, with nightmares or hallucinations, fever and what Susan considered to be pneumonia. Both mental and physical conditions required the best cure, in the form of his mother's constant care, nursing and reassurance, and it took him time to recover. The general effect of low spirits and depression at his uncertain future represented a very unhappy adolescent crisis. Life in Mahim must have been somewhat uncomfortable for the whole family, for Wilfred was in low health for some weeks and there was inevitable anxiety over his future. He had turned against his life-long religious beliefs, making a complete break with any possible career in the church. Yet again, he faced an uncertain future which depended on personal determination and unremitting, independent study.

It was unfortunate that at the same time Harold was also at home with no defined future, so that Tom and Susan had all their children dependent on them and both the two older boys unhappy and unemployed. Harold's studies at the Art School had started well but, as he had no hope of passing the qualifying examination to become a pupil-teacher, he had to give up the course and could not find local work. Mary was an essential support to Susan in running the house and Colin was making quiet progress at school; but neither of the two older boys could currently help with the hard-pressed household finances.

As always, Susan felt that religious guidance would help Wilfred and tried her best to provide it. However, it gradually became clear that the evangelical approach encouraged both at home and in Dunsden was a large part of the problem. Revd Wigan was deeply distressed by his young assistant's apparent shortcomings, but Wilfred's increasing awareness of other ideals and subtleties in human nature were clearly incompatible with Wigan's own strict faith and drive for religious revival.

In Shrewsbury there was a by-election in 1913, following the death of the local MP. This may have set off some heated discussions between Tom (a Conservative by instinct with experience of union activity on the railways) and his eldest son, with his recent insights into rural poverty and class divisions. The debate in Shrewsbury reflected the developing state of national politics: the Liberal candidate was strongly in favour of women's suffrage, but the main suffragist party was not supporting Liberal party candidates and so he withdrew. A local independent candidate was found, but was unable to defeat the Conservative candidate. There was, of course, no vote for Susan and other women for several years to come.

By April, Wilfred felt robust once more and had rediscovered his sense of humour. His final restoration to full health was completed when he and Colin visited relatives in Torquay where sea air and swimming completed the cure. There was a further reason to feel well and cheerful when he pursued his devotion to Keats's poetry with a pilgrimage to the poet's house in Teignmouth. This caused, as he said in a letter home, some bewilderment for the occupants, as he stood outside and peered at the house.

From his constant and careful reading, and the Dunsden experience, he had reached a sense that poets must speak out against oppression, and his self-imposed apprenticeship continued to lead him to deeper truths in poetry. His experiments with technique and control of language show him seeking constant recognition of human nature and better forms of expression. Recognising the importance of finding a new way through to adult life, he settled down to his books again and applied for the scholarship at Reading – but he had very little hope of passing.

The 'scandal' of Wilfred's departure from Dunsden seems to have died down at once, and he was warmly welcomed back on a visit later in the year. Nor did he entirely give up attendance at church, for his years of concentration on religious belief could not easily be eradicated; but it changed from depending on a particular pattern of devotion into a view of Christianity as one way among many in the search for faith, with imagination, human understanding and his own philosophy.

4 TRANSITIONS
I have my foothold

Looking back over more than a hundred years, the marks of change in 1913 Britain are clear to see. Unrest in the political and industrial worlds was considerable, with continual anxiety and debate about Ireland, and a major industrial strike in the Midlands. The suffragette movement was gathering pace. Lloyd George's new house suffered an arson attack and Emily Wilding Davison died when she ran in front of the King's horse in the Derby. The first female magistrate was appointed, and fifty thousand women marched and met in Hyde Park. On a different level of activity, which would affect Shrewsbury and the Owen family more directly, the Royal Flying Corps established the first British military airfield for fixed-wing aircraft, and in 1916 Monkmoor Airfield would be developed in the quiet fields beyond Cherry Orchard.

In Shrewsbury, the most visible sense of fresh commercial activity probably came from the rebirth in June 1911 of the old Potteries, Shrewsbury & North Wales railway line from Llanymynech to Shrewsbury. This was under the direction of an energetic civil engineer and later army officer, Colonel Stephens. Now called the Shropshire & Montgomeryshire Light Railway, by 1912 it provided mainly passenger services. It was a brave venture, using refurbished old rolling stock and locomotives, and running somewhat irregularly; but it served an impressive number of small rural communities.

The major reconstruction operations, followed by the noise, bustle, smoke and steam at the old railway premises and tracks opposite the Abbey, would be unavoidable for anyone passing the Abbey or going down Coleham Head and Belle Vue from the English Bridge. As a railway venture it was presumably a topic of conversation for Tom and his colleagues at Shrewsbury Station, but otherwise it probably remained outside the attention of the Owen family.

Other activities developed in this open level ground, including garages – and, in 1915, a world 'first' appeared near the Dun Cow pub near the Abbey, in the form of the first kerb-side petrol pump for the growing numbers of cars. Other transport facilities appeared and disappeared along Abbey Foregate and around the railway marshalling yards near the Carriage Works, together with premises by the road where bulk goods could be delivered for small-scale local delivery. Heavy lorries, coaches and hire cars were available for hire and organised outings became popular.

On the domestic scale, the Owen household faced the needs of two young sons who needed to step out into the adult world of work. Harold had left the Art School without completing his studies and now, at 16, could not find work in Shrewsbury. He hung around the house while knowing that he must make a bolder move. Susan Owen may perhaps have recalled her much-loved brother, Edward Shaw. He had been an extreme and wilful example of youthful uncertainty, who had profoundly shocked his father with his wild behaviour and disgraced his name in Oswestry. Circumstances and personalities in the Owen household were very different, but his disgrace and sudden departure to the United States had been a severe shock, leaving Susan in a state of enduring grief.

Harold, however, found a solution which echoed his father's youthful wishes, recalling Tom's earlier experience working his sea passage to India in his bachelor days. Fulfilling this frustrated ambition by proxy, Harold departed to Liverpool and signed on with the merchant navy, embarking on a hard and dangerous life which took him to places and experiences that he could not describe to his mother. His first trip, also to India, ended in near-disaster as he suffered severe heat stroke and had to return home to his mother's nursing and care. As he recovered, his stories of life at sea and in India – no doubt embellished by brotherly hints at the kind of low-life experience that would have shocked their parents – aroused Wilfred's envy, and his own shame at the failure of the Dunsden engagement. Ironically, in his later life, Harold returned to his original childhood instincts for art and design and became a proficient and modestly successful artist.

We know very little about the pattern of daily life in the Owen household and the atmosphere in which Susan's two older sons recovered their health in her care. It is clear that Susan was at the heart of all domestic activity, and that Mary was her chief support, messenger and assistant. Very little information has survived about mundane matters such as food or clothing. Harold's memoirs refer to 'delicious' dishes on special occasions, but Wilfred has nothing to say about meals beyond noting the sophistication that he first encountered in Dunsden Vicarage. It was not considered good manners to talk about food – on the other hand, Wilfred very frequently discusses his health, or his mother's, to an extent that in itself could seem unhealthy. Given the levels of smoke and dirt that were inescapable in any household, domestic help of some kind was essential, particularly when Susan was away and the family needed someone to prepare meals and maintain the daily routine.

One of Susan's chief concerns was the family's clothing, and as Tom's parents had worked in tailoring and clothing, the Owen children were brought up to pay

Fig. 48 *A platform of the Shropshire & Montgomeryshire Light Railway, with LNWR wagons and people boarding what may be an excursion train of four carriages, with the Abbey beyond (early twentieth century).*

careful attention to what they wore and how they behaved. Darning and mending was an inescapable part of domestic routine and Susan often made clothes for the family. Although they were all always neat and well turned-out, she retained her own extremely modest and discreet style of dress, and considered the use of cosmetics as socially unacceptable. Her attitudes can be perceived in her warnings to her sons about the dangers of sophisticated women.

July 1913 was a difficult month. While Harold was occupying Susan's attention before he could return to sea, Wilfred's pessimism over the Reading University College scholarship proved to be justified and the formal communication of his failure confirmed his darkest expectations. After Dunsden and his spell of ill health he had recognised the lack of time to prepare for the examination as he would have wished; but nonetheless it came as a very hard blow. His ambitions and the encouragement of his tutors and lecturers at Reading were no help. The failure here left him with no definite hope of employment, except for the despised career as an elementary teacher. Even this had its difficulties, for he would need a further matriculation pass (in geography) together with a 'primary student' college place – and would have to commit himself to teaching for a minimum of seven years. Whatever happened, he

Andrew Hunter

MANCHESTER
AND
SHREWSBURY

FOUND IN FATHER'S POCKETBOOK

could not expect any further financial support from his long-suffering parents. It was at this period of disappointment and unsatisfied ambition that he and Stanley Webb encountered the Oxford archaeologists at Uriconium, underlining the significance of the higher education that seemed destined to evade him.

Perhaps stirred by Harold's success in leaving home and finding employment, Wilfred looked again at the advertisements that often appeared in teaching magazines, seeking teachers of English for schools overseas. He remembered how much he had enjoyed his two holidays in Brittany with Tom a few years earlier – real fluency in French would be a considerable advantage and he could sit for the Reading scholarship again in a year's time. As an undertaking it would also be a good way to leave home, his family and Shrewsbury, and assert his adult independence.

In August Wilfred visited Tom's sister Emmie and her husband Edward Quayle in Wallasey, not far from his childhood city of Birkenhead. Here, he found lively young cousins, tennis and general social activity. Back home again he wrote to his cousin Leslie about the flowers on display at Shrewsbury Flower Show (always a great annual occasion), where he considered everything – flowers, music, fireworks and acrobats – at least up to expectations. Both there and at the Quayles' comfortable house and large garden he was intrigued by the names of roses and their sweetness. As implied in a poem enclosed in the letter to Leslie Gunston in mid-August, these reflections led him on to hints of imagined pleasures, dreams and veiled hints at love and possession. The strong sense of his delight in this rich poetic language cannot quite conceal his lack of adult experience and emotions:

> *When late I viewed the gardens of rich men,*
> *Where throve my darling blossoms plenteously ...*
> *... I keep them young.*
>
> *But when more spacious pleasances I trod,*
> *And saw their thousand buds, but might not kiss*
> *Though loving like a lover ...*
> *Sad was the yearning of my avarice.*
>
> *...*

Wilfred's letter to Leslie enclosing the sonnet describes it as barely 'worth your reading' – perhaps his cousin shared his frustrations at their lack of the sophistication to sustain such expressions as 'loving like a lover'. The letter was sent in mid-August, and gave no hint of his plans. His next surviving communication was also to his cousin, and came from Bordeaux in mid-September. He had taken the route which

Fig. 49 (left) *Portrait photograph of Midshipman Harold Owen (1915 / 1917).*

was to be familiar to many students in the later decades of the twentieth century, and was now engaged on teaching English as a foreign language in the local Berlitz School. The pay was low and he was constantly short of money, but he found acceptable lodgings and relished the experience of living in a large and handsome historic city, enjoying the atmosphere and activity in the streets and docks, and the range of pupils he encountered in each busy week. Letters home show him gaining confidence in his own independence and abilities, and taking great pleasure in his encounters with a new culture and fresh friends. There was nothing to keep him in Shrewsbury now apart from his family; but for Susan to see the departure of the son on whom she had consistently lavished such loving care and hopes must have been difficult.

In October Tom travelled to Bordeaux to see how his eldest son was getting on – a visit which led to a thoroughly embarrassing moment for both father and son. Conscious of his situation at the heart of one of France's greatest cities, teaching mostly adults on an individual basis and enjoying their cultured and sociable company, Wilfred quickly acquired friends and a good social life. Reluctant to explain the modesty of the Owen household, he had been somewhat evasive about his father's employment – and the implication, never directly contradicted, had developed easily amongst these new French friends that the father of young Professeur Owen held a title of some kind, perhaps as a baronet, and that he himself was waiting to go to Oxford University. Faced with his father's presence in the city, Wilfred struggled to explain the situation to him and Tom immediately assumed that he was trying to confess to some relationship or entanglement with a girl. He was perhaps much relieved to learn the snobbish but harmless truth and played the part well. Father and son had an extremely happy week together.

The strong ties with home were sustained by letters and, as ever, descriptions of various minor ailments, such as a chest infection and strained voice made worse by a timetable that often included evening classes as well as a full day. His pupils included a medical student who invited Wilfred to watch surgical operations in Bordeaux Hospital, and another, an advocate, who invited him to attend sessions in the law courts. Wilfred had to change lodgings to save money, but found that he was enjoying the work and could manage the system of teaching English to his French students entirely through the use of English. Back in his lodgings in the evening he heard the many church bells ringing irregularly across the city and thought how different they were from the familiar change-ringing in England. By the end of the year he had discovered the Union Protestant hostel for cheap meals and a warm common room with a piano, attended the chapel of a local Protestant hospital, and once accompanied friends to midnight Mass in the cathedral. Otherwise, he had escaped from the more rigid routines of established church attendance.

In the spring of 1914, Wilfred was still intending to try once again for the Reading

University College scholarship in the coming summer, and spent what time he could on studying, as well as experimenting with poetry. At the end of January he enjoyed the traditional Students' Ball, with fine decorations, music and dancing, and a good deal of flirtation and high spirits – as unlike Dunsden twelve months earlier as could be imagined. Susan evidently worried about Wilfred, and warned him against women who would be attracted to him, but he assured her that he was well able to ignore such temptations.

Writing home a few days before his 21st birthday in March 1914, Wilfred expressed his motto as: 'Never do anything today if it can possibly be done tomorrow' – which sounds very unlike his intensive studying but perhaps reflects his uncertainty about what to do next in life. The day brought long and loving letters, and presents from his family which suited his interests: a handsome fountain pen from his parents, a fine copy of Shelley's collected poetry from his siblings, and a small book of Tennyson's work from his cousin Leslie.

At this time, his family set Wilfred the task of finding a boy of about Colin's age who would visit Shrewsbury to improve his English. This was not simple, but in the end he proposed Raoul Lem, from a Protestant family whose situation was reasonably similar to the Owen household. After setting up the contact, Wilfred became somewhat disturbed by seeing more of Raoul and recognising the boy's immaturity; but the visit to Shrewsbury went ahead in the summer of 1914.

Susan Owen might well have regretted the idea, for the international experiment was not a success. Raoul, an only child, turned out to be self-centred and ill-prepared for the bustle, constant discussion and general style of the Owen household. It took all of Susan's strength of purpose and determination to get him to behave more or less sensibly and take notice of what she told him, or required him to do. Harold later described Raoul as 'thoroughly spoilt' as well as disobedient, wildly emotional and extremely demonstrative. Raoul was determined to show off on the horses grazing unattended on the old racecourse, and by swimming in the river. But despite his boasting of prowess at both, it turned out that he could neither ride at all nor swim competently. Instead, he incited the horses to buck and bolt when Colin was riding, and nearly drowned in the river because he could barely swim.

The most alarming incident occurred when Raoul insisted on picking and eating wild fungi. He became extremely ill, which caused uproar in the household and required the expense and worry of a doctor's visit. At a less dramatic level, Wilfred had indicated to his mother ahead of the visit that Raoul's reliability and behaviour were somewhat suspect, and warned her that the boy must on no account be allowed to use Wilfred's bicycle as he would assuredly damage it. Wilfred recognised that he had been unwise to set up the contact, but maintained good relations with the Lem family, who continued to be kind to him in Bordeaux.

By the early summer of 1914 Wilfred had discarded the possibility of retaking the Reading scholarship examination and the prospect of elementary teaching. He half-planned to take a course at Bordeaux University, but had come to no conclusion. In the meantime, there was a rural visit to relatives of the Lem family, and here he recorded for the first time the flutters of emotion caused by a young girl with beautiful eyes – Henriette Poitou was only sixteen, but she evidently disturbed Wilfred's equanimity. However, he was more conscious of his young French companion's agitation and desperate wish to draw Henriette's attention to himself. As Wilfred wrote to his sister Mary:

> *For my part I could only sit like an Egyptian piece of Statuary, hands on knees, staring apparently into space; but seeing well enough to count how often the marvellous eyes looked in my direction, which was exactly four times per minute. Finally, Raoul made a complete ass of himself, and H. fled from the table, and locked herself up for half an hour.*

Such words would reassure his sister – who would automatically share the letter with her mother.

In France, a distant event in June 1914 did not immediately appear to be of world importance, and the shooting of the Austrian Archduke Franz Ferdinand in Sarajevo soon dropped out of the headlines in the Bordeaux newspapers. Of greater interest to the Owen family was an invitation to Wilfred to spend six weeks on a working holiday in the foothills of the Pyrenees. The suggestion came from one of his pupils, Madame Léger, an elegant business woman, a Parisian whose rather older husband had given up engineering to concentrate on acting and the arts. Both she and her 11-year-old daughter Nénette would be tutored in English, and Wilfred would have plenty of time to enjoy the summer season in the fashionable spa town of Bagnères-de-Bigorre. At the end of July Wilfred gave in his notice to leave the Berlitz School. He had no fixed idea of what he might do after his long summer break, beyond the realisation that he could always find work as a teacher of English.

In Shrewsbury, as the world was beginning to take notice of new and alarming challenges, King George V took time to spend a day out in Shrewsbury early in July. It was an important occasion for Tom Owen to ensure that the smoothest and smartest possible greeting should be ready at an impeccable station. The King set off through the streets in his horse-drawn carriage with a military escort, through massed crowds and to great acclaim. Security and protection were very tight, in view of national disturbances (primarily over Ireland), and also the continuing suffragette activities.

Fig. 50 *Royal visit of King George V in Shrewsbury, 3 July 1914. An open carriage drive for King George V, watched by large crowds as he is greeted by civic dignitaries in The Square. He then opened the West Midland Agricultural Show (on the old racecourse on Monkmoor Road) and also bestowed the title 'Royal' on the Salop Infirmary (1914).*

The King's principal duty was to visit the Royal Agricultural Show, held on the old Racecourse, close to the Owens' house in Monkmoor Road. Its former main building still survived from the old days of racing, a fine mock-timbered pavilion with gables and a larger central section, which provided a pleasing backdrop for the royal visit. Flags were flying on the turrets, and local enterprise was visible on the wooden fences round the central grassed area, where a large notice proclaimed: 'Royal Show Ground. This Valuable Building Estate 56 Acres to be Sold', with more mock Tudor for the offices close by.

It is impossible to know whether Wilfred would have been swept up in the general excitement, or remained aloof, but in his absence Mary, Harold and Colin made the most of the day. Their neighbour and close friend Mary Ragge was with them, and noted that they 'followed the King around all day'. Photographs and a short news film show King George V emerging from the station and being driven through the streets past massed crowds, inspecting a line of military veterans (including a Chelsea Pensioner), as well as a line-up of winning cattle, which included his own prize-winning black Dexter bull.

This may have been the occasion for a display of specially-constructed model farm buildings to show how farm workers could be well-housed in low-cost accommodation; and two years later the old racecourse was used as a camp for soldiers who were engaged in helping with harvest work.

During those summer days in late-July and early-August, one nation after another declared war in a sequence of terse statements, and men were mobilised in their thousands in the countries directly concerned. More disturbing to civilian families and employers in Britain at that stage was the ensuing appeal for large numbers of volunteers: Britain's small standing army was far too small to meet her immediate commitment to defend Belgium in a continental war.

In the Owen family, Tom was the person most immediately affected by the onset of war, since railway timetables and organisation were disrupted and he was likely to lose workmen at a particularly difficult time. The rail services would be under great pressure, as Shrewsbury was an important centre with large numbers of troops to be billeted in the town. Horses and carts or wagons, cars and lorries were requisitioned for permanent or temporary army use. In Crewe, where many engine drivers, firemen

Fig. 51 *Model farm cottages built of concrete blocks to demonstrate good housing for agricultural workers at a modest price, on show as a commercial venture at the 1914 Royal Agricultural Show (1914).*

Fig. 52 *Staff at the Royal Show on the old racecourse, Shrewsbury. Workmen in front of a large medallion depicting Britannia. The board is marked 'L and N.W. Ry Royal Show Staff Shrewsbury 1914' for the London & North Western Railway (1914).*

and fitters volunteered for war service, their railway employers guaranteed to keep their jobs open and pay their wives and families up to ten shillings a week.

In mid-August the Shrewsbury Police Court charged a Sheffield journalist with being in a prohibited area of the L&NW and GW Joint Railways' railway tracks. The man had been living in Shrewsbury since the royal visit a month earlier, had made sketches of local railway bridges, and had apparently written letters to newspapers about the highly contentious matter of Irish Home Rule. Supposed 'spies' were imagined to be everywhere, and three motorists (an Englishman, a Russian and a German) were arrested, interrogated and subsequently released. On 8 August, the Light Infantry was mobilising at the Barracks in Copthorne Road, strengthened by 500 army reservists, while gangs of workmen installed lavatories under the old Market Hall in the Square for troops gathering before their departure. Lord Kitchener was calling for another 100,000 volunteers.

At the domestic level there were reports of rising costs and panic buying, and much domestic and official time was taken up with fund-raising. The Mayor of Shrewsbury declared his support for the Prince of Wales' National War Relief Fund, seeking practical cooperation and distribution of money and support. Local committees were

Fig. 53 *Villa Lorenzo. Wilfred spent several happy weeks in the foothills of the Pyrenees in the summer of 1914. Amid the dazzling scenery he enjoyed his first encounters with intellectually-minded people and worked at his own poetry.*

Fig. 54 *At a reading at the casino, Bagnères-de-Bigorre. In the spa town, Wilfred (front row, moustache, bow tie and soft hat) sits next to Madame Léger, his elegant hostess in white on his left, and her daughter Nénette, his pupil (1914).*

formed with a wide variety of aims, and potential convalescent homes were organised. Proposals were offered to improve local garden produce by distributing vegetable seeds, and help for the dependants of men who had left for the war or for men thrown out of work because of the conflict.

Very soon refugees began to arrive from Belgium as thousands of people fled from the destruction of their homes and nation. Funds were raised all over Britain and accommodation prepared. At one point in October, 16,000 people arrived in Folkestone in desperate and immediate need. In Shrewsbury the old Armoury, near the Column, was prepared and opened to take in families, and a local businessman rushed to Belgium to collect his young daughter from school.

At home in Monkmoor Road, Colin Owen was still at school, too young to be involved – yet – and Harold was already actively at sea in the merchant navy. At the same time, in the midst of the descent into war, Wilfred set out from Bordeaux to spend six weeks in the foothills of the Pyrenees, living in a delightful villa with fine mountain views and surrounded by beautiful open countryside and streams. He was met at the station by M. Léger and his daughter Nénette, with a donkey cart to carry his luggage the short distance out of the town to the Villa Lorenzo.

His establishment with the Léger family must have delighted Susan Owen, for Wilfred had taken pains to describe Monsieur and Madame Léger to her, emphasising their style and sophistication, with a very active and varied social life. Susan's only concern was that Nénette might attract Wilfred's attention too strongly, but he assured her again that he was immune to such charms. Although he was open to a range of distractions in such a household, he was there to work, since Madame Léger must improve her English before a planned business trip to England.

This was the month when Raoul Lem was staying in Shrewsbury, and it must have been particularly irritating for his parents, as they struggled with their awkward visitor, to think of Wilfred enjoying his interesting and sophisticated engagement as part of a prosperous family holiday. On the other hand, he was safely removed from the inescapable evidence of military activity which surrounded even such a devout and peace-loving household as Mahim.

In the gathering atmosphere of general anxiety and alarm, it was impossible to ignore the Drill Hall in Coleham, originally set up for the 1st Shropshire Rifle Volunteer corps and opened in 1881. Next to the Hall, a Riding School was built in 1911 on the former site of William Hazledine's timber yard, for the use of both the Royal Horse Artillery and the Shropshire Yeomanry. The presence of military activity and the sight of uniformed soldiers and horsemen were normal features of the street scene to an extent almost unimaginable a century later – but the bustle of recruitment, equipping, drilling and then despatching troops by train was far more intense.

In September the news from the Pyrenees was distinctly unwarlike, although Wilfred had to obtain a permit to be in France and to prove that he was not a French shirker avoiding his military duty. Most local men had already disappeared to rejoin their army units and the women spent their time sitting at their street door and knitting.

Wilfred's own view of the war was remarkably detached and he expressed himself somewhat disdainfully, stating to his mother that the guns would 'effect a little useful weeding', perhaps revealing the senses of a very young man overwhelmed by nature and beauty. War was not for him, he felt; better to write to the fullest extent of his mind than to be one of the crowd of volunteers rushing to enlist. We do not know what Susan wrote to him about the war, but the insistence on the heroic approach to war in his younger reading, and the Englishman's 'duty to enlist and join the conflict', seems to have aroused his own sense of independence; the urgent demands of 'patriotism' and 'duty' evidently did not recall his early essay-writing on 'Leadership' and 'England' at Birkenhead Institute. As he was absorbing the atmosphere of his sophisticated companions and the mountain landscape where he spent six happy weeks that summer, his eyes were opened to the world on a larger scale.

Before leaving for the Légers' holiday house, Wilfred visited a Bordeaux photographer and was pleased with the result, describing to his mother his fine healthy colour, and the chic effect of his moustache. It seems clear that Wilfred's looks and style in this fashionable summer season fitted in very well with French ideas, and he was by now becoming quite a dandy. Parting his hair down the centre of his head looks somewhat unexpected to modern viewers, but there is no doubt that he had developed a steady, firm gaze – as seen again in later photographs in uniform. Harold, a good observer, was aware of his brother's 'secret' smile, an expression of his inward ideas of the world and other people.

Wilfred's plans and hopes had often been thwarted, or had shown to be impractical, but in some ways he seems to have made his own luck. Even the Dunsden episode had shown him where he had made a false start and had in the end stimulated him to make the final and conclusive break from his mother's side. Now, in the relaxed and entrancing surroundings of the Pyrenees, he found the next step along his way to fulfilling his long-held wish to be a poet: at last, he found himself in the midst of creative and literary-minded people who encouraged and stimulated his thinking.

The most significant figure among the Légers' friends was a well-known poet and writer from Paris, Laurent Tailhade, who was delighted to talk with this keen young Englishman and made quite a fuss over him. This was Wilfred's first encounter with an active, published writer and man of letters; his introduction to French writers whose work would not become familiar in his Shrewsbury circles

Fig. 55 (right) *Wilfred's first literary contact, Laurent Tailhade. A well-known poet of the day, he encouraged Wilfred during the holiday and subsequently (1914).*

for many years to come. Some of them, such as Rimbaud, Verlaine and Baudelaire, influenced Wilfred's own work considerably, and added to the many sources which can be traced in his mature writing.

Wilfred was now in a curious situation, whether or not he was fully aware of it: both Madame Léger and her young daughter found him attractive, and now this well-known poet and man of letters was pressing compliments and encouragement on him. This attention from people whom he liked and admired was all very pleasant, but any one of these relationships could easily have drawn him into all sorts of complication. Susan Owen's suspicions had been aroused by his descriptions of Madame Léger and her elegance. Susan herself was intensely cautious and modest in all matters of dress and style, and had always warned her son to be wary of feminine attractions. Perhaps in response to these precautionary words, Wilfred declared his own caution, and also declined a suggestion from his employer that the young tutor should accompany her on a business trip to Canada, all expenses paid … He refused to be drawn in by any of the three and he remained on cordial good terms with everyone.

In his notebook for that summer Wilfred began a technical exercise in wordplay and picture-building – not concerned with his frequent searches for deep emotional expression or imagined exploration of literary romance, but full of the observed land-scape and the deliberate expression of the effect on his feelings and thoughts. These pages are well-known now for his expression of pararhyme, when 'Leaves …' is half-rhymed with 'Lives …' and 'Stirs …' with 'Stars …', the words together building up a flickering image of the living landscape.

It was a life beyond anything that Shrewsbury could offer, or that he could fully explain to his mother, particularly against the background of imminent warfare and all its preparations. He knew that Harold was away at sea again, Mary had become a voluntary nurse, Colin (still a schoolboy), was in the Scouts, and Tom was giving his energies as a part-time volunteer – so that the whole of the household was engaged in civilian activities associated with the war.

After his return to Bordeaux, Wilfred wrote to Harold and included some pencil drawings of soldiers' wounds (a doctor friend had invited Wilfred to visit the wards and see men who had been sent from the front for operations and treatment). For his brother's education, as he states, there were some gruesome descriptions to accompany the illustrations, and descriptions of the damage and treatment. By now, a French min-istry was occupying university premises in Bordeaux, and the city was heavily crowded.

From the very outset of the war, Shrewsbury witnessed the consequences of con-flict on the continent. There was naturally a great increase in military visibility in the town. The local newspapers carried news of casualties as well as battles fought, and from the earliest days there were news items on food shortages. The first group of Belgian refugees reached Shrewsbury on 19 September, with a larger number in late

October who had taken 12 days to travel from Ostend to London. Accommodation was provided in the hastily refurbished former Armoury building between the London and Much Wenlock roads, with appeals for furniture and equipment of every kind for domestic use.

For wounded soldiers, houses all over the country were made available to be run as nursing homes, with VAD (Voluntary Aid Detachment) staff. Oakley Manor in Belle Vue, and Prestfelde House in London Road, were typical of many throughout the country and became an essential part of the national response to the war. For many women it was the counterpart to their menfolk's absence at the front, providing practical help at a time when large numbers of wounded men were arriving and needed care of all kinds, sometimes for long periods. At the same time, women at home were constantly knitting to provide socks and other clothing for the troops – for one of their own family, a friend or anyone in need. Endless committees organised, raised funds, distributed parcels, supported families, and did what they could on the home front. In the longer term, volunteer work of this kind turned into the basis for an enduring professional life and an alternative to domesticity.

Fig. 56 *Wounded soldiers convalescing in Shrewsbury. Oakley Hospital in Belle Vue was used as a VAD (Voluntary Aid Detachment) hospital which depended on its many local volunteers. A special 'Hospital Blue' uniform was supplied for patients to identify their military status (c.1916).*

Another demand on local attention was the camp for German prisoners that appeared in the old railway yard area opposite the Abbey, in the now empty premises of the old Midland Railway Wagon and Carriage Works. The buildings were in a primitive state and not suitable for accommodation, with leaking roofs and beaten earth floors, but with improvements they became acceptable. Civilians, now enemy aliens, came first, and were soon followed by prisoners of war, who arrived with nothing except the uniforms they were wearing at the moment of capture. Towards Christmas 1914 there was local anxiety (to some extent driven by newspaper articles) over proposals for the prisoners to hold a fund-raising concert in order to buy small personal items. It was felt by some local people that these enemies in their midst should not be supported in this way, and the project was abandoned, to the great distress of the retired army officer responsible for their custody. In a published letter to the Mayor of Shrewsbury he expressed his regret and noted that the men of the National Reserve, who were guarding the prisoners, had been the first to buy tickets.

Fig. 57 *German prisoner-of-war camp. Now hidden under supermarket premises, the site is defined by the railway embankment arches on the left and the Abbey visible in the background, beyond the prisoners' washing lines. One of the prisoners is a sailor, wearing the German Kriegsmarine uniform (c.1916).*

The recreation area was not large, but by the end of 1916 the camp had concrete floors, a sick bay, washing facilities and latrines, and prisoners had taken up boot-making, tailoring and making small items for sale. The number of inmates grew to over 560 by the end of 1916 and they had created a vegetable garden to improve their own diet. Later, as the shortage of manpower became desperate, prisoner work parties were sent out daily by train from Shrewsbury to work in local farms and quarries. Although Shrewsbury was far from the front line, the prisoners close to the Abbey were a constant reminder of front line events, and awareness of the conflict was inescapable.

Meanwhile, on Wilfred's return to Bordeaux he was dismayed to find that the French War Ministry had taken over the university premises, and the Berlitz School had closed for lack of custom. Rather than admit defeat and go home, he decided to stay and seek pupils wanting private tuition. Initially he lodged with the Légers in their elegant house in an exclusive part of the city, while he contacted previous acquaintances and looked for pupils. This was when he was taken round the temporary military hospital with his doctor friend, to see the conditions and wounds. His letters home at this point show no sign of future attitude to the war; evidently, personal experience would be very different from the observation of other people's plight. He found a few pupils in Bordeaux – just enough to encourage him to stay – and carried on teaching; and had now reached the point where he could tell Susan of the intelligence and range of his friends and acquaintances compared with her circles in Shrewsbury.

The international conflict was, by now, creating growing uncertainty in Wilfred's mind. He was already anxious and confused about his own future, given the lack of funds available for the level of education he longed for. Yet he recognised that his own poetic leanings were well-founded. In March 1915 he wrote to his mother:

> To some, I seem a fellow without a footing in life. But I have my foothold,
> bold as any, kept for years. A boy, I guessed that the fullest, largest liveable
> life was that of a Poet. I know it now ...

At this point Wilfred fortunately gained a new pupil via the British Consul. The man was a member of a distinguished local French family who was employed by the British in China, was married to an Englishwoman, and whose four boys could not return to their English school because of the dangers of crossing the Channel. A retired family governess was teaching the younger two, but Wilfred was asked to teach the older two until they could all cross the Channel in safety.

Wilfred moved out to the house at Mérignac, just outside Bordeaux, where the boys were staying in the governess's house. His board and lodging were provided by the family, and after taking the tram into Bordeaux each morning to teach his pupils there he returned to supervise all four boys in the afternoons, often with their friends, in the gardens and local estates. In the early evening there was an intensive teaching session with the older boys. It was a very comfortable pattern, and thoughts of the war intruded very little, beyond dismay when his hero, the French flying ace Roland Garros, was shot down. By the spring of 1915 he was thinking more deeply about his future, but without any firm conclusion beyond the assertion that his early ambitions to be a poet must be pursued.

In May 1915 he was briefly back in England on behalf of a Bordeaux business friend who wanted representation at a trade exhibition in London. There was time for a short visit to Shrewsbury, but barely long enough to feel settled there – perhaps with some fresh reflections on how the war was affecting his own country while he was living in distant Bordeaux, far from the front line. France had suffered particularly severely in the battles of 1914, but military service was universal, obligatory and automatic, and the absence of most men was the natural consequence of war. Meanwhile the British Army was also suffering very considerable losses. The British civilian population was generally unaccustomed to military matters, but with the outbreak of war large numbers of young men from all kinds of labouring, commercial or professional life were responding to the call for volunteers. This expression of patriotic fervour in his home country was striking for Wilfred after his months of growing independence and immersion in the French language, culture and ideas.

While in London that spring, Wilfred had time to visit the Royal Academy and take an evening walk around the East End, which found its way into his poetry, a vision of dangerous youthful beauty in the great city. Susan Owen's eldest sister, Mary, had married a doctor and they lived and worked in the East End. Although she died when quite young, Wilfred visited the family and was fascinated by the area with its crowds of foreign seamen, the trading wealth, the poverty and the exotic-looking refugees in this multilingual world of the working Thames. A poem written in 1918 evokes the mysteries of the river and its tides:

> *I am the ghost of Shadwell Stair.*
> *Along the wharves by the water-house,*
> *And through the cavernous slaughter-house,*
> *I am the shadow that walks there.*

By now he was becoming confident in his ability to hint at secret knowledge, at intimate or hidden experience.

The turbulent political atmosphere at this time was inescapable, and Wilfred attended a patriotic meeting at the Guildhall where Herbert Asquith, the Prime Minister, called for support to strengthen national determination. The Minister

Fig. 58 *This howitzer and truck, photographed in 1934, confirm Longden Coleham's military past. The dilapidated building behind, with its handsome entrance, was once a cotton factory. It was later demolished.*

for War, Lord Kitchener, made his call for another 300,000 men to add to the vast numbers of volunteers who had joined up since the summer of 1914. Recruiting posters were prominent everywhere – and there was a notice in his hotel stating that, subject to age and fitness, any 'gentleman returning from abroad' could obtain a commission with the Artists' Rifles. As he was not enthusiastic at the thought of serving in the ranks, and the normal requirement for voluntary enlistment as an officer was based on family background and a public school (Shrewsbury Borough Technical School was not on the list of 'acceptable' schools), the Artists' Rifles held some appeal.

Wilfred returned to Bordeaux, conscious now of his own youthful patriotism (and perhaps recalling his school essays long ago) – not so much for the abstract concept of country but rather for the inherited culture that was such an essential part of his thinking and well-being. Although it was a great pleasure to be back in Bordeaux and

Figs. 59 & 60 (overleaf) *Two portrait photographs of Wilfred taken by his uncle John Gunston. Despite appearances, both were probably taken in the same year, 1915. The first (on left) shows a slightly self-conscious young man back from France, with bow tie and centre parting. The second (on right) shows the same man grinning, in his first uniform as an officer cadet in the Artists' Rifles.*

teaching, he was very conscious of his change of attitude towards the war. Perhaps it was only in France, right away from his family (however much he wrote to them and thought about his life in Shrewsbury), that he could go on to tell his mother in a letter in June:

> *I don't want the bore of training, I don't want to wear khaki; or yet to save my honour before inquisitive grand-children fifty years hence. But I <u>now do</u> most <u>intensely want to fight</u>.*

During the following month, Wilfred's letters expressed his wish to seek a commission. By mid-July, he felt that if he was unsuccessful in being taken on in the Artists' Rifles for officer training, '... I should like to join the Italian Army'; and in his next letter a week later, in apparent reference to an expression of doubt from his mother, he commented, '... The Commission might be very long in coming. I seriously should like to join the Italian Cavalry; for reasons both aesthetic and practical ...' But in a postscript to this letter he remarked on three notable figures – the well-known artists Lord Leighton and Sir John Millais, and Sir John Forbes-Robertson, an actor and theatrical manager – who had all been in the Artists' Rifles. Evidently it was the delay after reaching his decision to enlist which drove him to consider alternatives. But the summer weeks passed pleasantly and energetically with the English boys. In September, the opportunity to accompany them back to England provided the final impetus to follow his decision. After the long journey, he was sad to say goodbye to them as he saw them off by train to their school – but he went straight to the Artists' Rifles Headquarters, was passed fit and was accepted as an officer cadet.

The next month was spent at home, where his parents were torn between anxiety at the dangers ahead and the certainty that he was doing the right thing. There had been some embarrassment at the long delay in what most of his family and friends assumed was an obvious decision, since friends such as Stanley Webb and the Bulmans had enlisted promptly. A round of visits took in his cousins, his helpful tutor Dr Morley in Reading, and the Timpanys, of the Technical School, in Shrewsbury – all of them sources from which he had received kindness and advice. Now, putting aside all his ideas of further travel and teaching, by the end of October 1915 Wilfred had become Private Owen, Number 4756, 28th London Regiment (Artists' Rifles). However unlikely it may have been, his belief in poetry as the representation of the human spirit, and his pressing determination to discover and express it, endured as his passport to the future.

5   DESTINATIONS
all a poet can do today is warn

B Y the time Wilfred made up his own mind to join the war, he had seen its effects on French families far from the front line, and had visited wounded soldiers under treatment in Bordeaux. We do not know how much Susan Owen discussed the war in her letters to Wilfred, although she must have felt the struggle between her religious beliefs and her instinctive patriotism. To have her eldest son living comfortably abroad and continuing with his teaching career there when his compatriots were volunteering to fight was probably a cause for embarrassment in Shrewsbury; and with Tom Owen's patriotic allegiance to crown and country it was natural to expect his son of military age to fight for his country.

Wilfred's brief visit to England in the spring of 1915 may have brought home to him what the war meant for Britain – or perhaps he simply preferred to make up his own mind and not feel under pressure to 'do the right thing'. Whatever the case, he was not enthusiastic at the thought of serving in the ranks, and was pleased to have found an opening where he could be taken on as an officer cadet. By the time he returned to Britain in September, with the heavy responsibility of conducting his young pupils from France to their English school, the war had been going on for more than a year and was clearly not going to end soon.

The need for ever more men in the British Army was obvious, and the very name of the Artists' Rifles, with their emblem of Mars and Minerva, was a considerable draw. The photograph taken by John Gunston of his nephew soon after enlistment shows a light-hearted beginner. In effect this was the moment, even more than the move to Bordeaux, which represented the final break from Shrewsbury and his parents' experience and influence. Life in the army was fresh, disconcerting and demanding, and the young officer cadet plunged into it cheerfully and willingly. Becoming an officer cadet with the Artists' Rifles confirmed his instinct to join a unit where his literary ambitions might find companionship. At their Drill Hall (still visible just off Euston Road, with the carved regimental badge of Mars and Minerva over the door), this

Fig. 61 *A group of men in uniform on a river outing from the Quarry. The hats of three women present appear to indicate their membership of Queen Alexandra's Imperial Military Nursing Service (c.1915).*

was his introduction to Bloomsbury, with all its creative implications – as well as to the army. In his off-duty hours he enjoyed wholeheartedly the sensation of being a young intellectual properly at home here.

The initial stages of learning military ways, the constant repetition of basic training and the physical discomforts and fatigue were all at first interesting to Wilfred, then tedious. Letters home describe the trials of typhoid inoculation and the mysteries of continual basic drill exercises. Learning how to give a smart salute provided some local entertainment, as the trees in nearby public gardens were used for practice. Through these early stages, Wilfred's letters express appreciation of the steadiness of the sergeants and their good humour in off-duty hours. The secrets of military clothing, the labour of polishing buttons and the difficulty of arranging puttees were balanced by an evident pleasure in the admiration of small boys or older residents when he went through the streets in uniform.

A more intellectual escape came during Wilfred's visits to the Poetry Bookshop, not far from the Drill Hall, where he could attend readings and refresh his literary thinking. The Bookshop, opened by Harold Monro in 1913 in Devonshire Street

Fig. 62 *Wilfred in training (front row, second from right). After enlistment and basic training, he was posted to The Manchesters for further training with the 5th Battalion (1916).*

(now Boswell Street), was an important focus for 'the Georgian poets'. The name emerged from Monro's own publication in 1912 of *Georgian Poetry*, an anthology reflecting the work of a group of modern writers who reacted against the somewhat florid writing of late Victorian poets and sought a straightforward and more everyday style of expression. As well as promoting new poetry, the shop held readings and became a recognised meeting place for modern-minded writers, particularly during the war years. Monro also provided a few rooms as lodgings above the shop, and Wilfred stayed there quite frequently when his training took him away from central London.

Next in his army career came the much larger and more impersonal establishment of Hare Hall Camp in Essex, where he discovered the monotony of being on guard duty and standing sentry for many hours, and where parcels from home were a welcome contrast to the realities of communal life. The steady routine of training here involved crowded barrack-hut accommodation, constant drill and lectures. Evenings were spent on preparing maps and reports – it was like being back at school again, with the added homework of constant chores to maintain military standards. It was hardly a poetic world, and one of the striking might-have-beens of the time was that although Edward Thomas was in the same camp at the same time, the two men never met and probably died without knowing each other's work.

In June 1916, Wilfred was commissioned into the Manchester Regiment and joined them as a junior officer at Witley and Aldershot. This new stage reminded him of past experience – a combination of what he recalled of life in Birkenhead and of his young pupils in the Wyle Cop School; their need to be cajoled and instructed. Most of the troops were Manchester and Lancashire men, described by Wilfred as '… hard-handed hard-minded miners, dogged, loutish, ugly …' – but he felt he could trust them. A month's course at Oswestry provided a wonderful opportunity to see his parents and recover a sense of home. Whatever embarrassment Susan and Tom may have felt in 1914, when so many Englishmen of his age were enlisting while Wilfred was safe in Bordeaux, was now swept away by seeing him in uniform, despite the vast casualty lists, and sad news from neighbours or distant friends.

It was an active time for all the Owen family. Mary was nursing and Colin spent the summer working on a farm near Shrewsbury. While Wilfred was at Witley Camp, he was visited by Harold, who, having been in the Merchant Navy since he was 14, was now about to join the Royal Naval Air Service. With both brothers now

Fig. 63 *A steam threshing machine on a farm near Cound, outside Shrewsbury, where Colin Owen worked before joining the RAF. During the First World War, troops and machinery were made available at harvest time to help sustain food supplies. One man is wearing a military cap (c.1916).*

independent adults and engaged in serving their country, they felt closer to each other than in their childhood years.

Second Lieutenant Wilfred Owen finally reached the Western Front with the 2nd Manchesters on New Year's Day, 1917, in what would turn out to be one of the coldest winters for many years. His first letter from France, written the same day, emphasised 'a fine heroic feeling' and a sense of excitement. This flourish of youthful defiance faded into resigned acceptance through the delays and discomforts of slow trains moving towards the front line, and the incessant chill of driving rain and inescapable mud. The drama of the situation, the drive to be a good officer, was balanced in his letters by mundane requests for minor personal needs.

Although Wilfred was now encountering troops and officers who had already spent long months on active service in France, he knew he was fully trained and was a fine shot with rifle or revolver. He felt ready to meet this new experience and to throw himself into it. The end of the Battle of the Somme had officially been declared in November 1916, but Wilfred was posted to a part of the original front line that had barely moved since the opening of the battle in July. Today, the British military cemeteries along this line define the area where Wilfred's battalion was posted in the continuing confrontation near Serre, south of Arras.

Although Wilfred Owen's periods of active service were brief, they were intense and profoundly significant in shaping his insights into the human spirit. Always a keen and attentive pupil, he had made good use of his months in training – but the incidents and dangers that met him in the cold, opening months of 1917 were far beyond the preparation of parade ground and firing range. Dunsden and Bordeaux had been stepping-stones along the way to achieving his ambitions, but modern warfare lay outside all previous imagining.

In time, most families came to understand that a great deal of the war was spent in waiting, confusion, discomfort, boredom and fatigue, with any or all of these accompanied by acute danger. Although the losses through death or injury were truly dreadful, and in some places affected whole communities at once when men had joined their local 'Pals' battalion, it took many decades before the nation as a whole understood the inhuman conditions. Millions of letters were delivered to waiting families through a remarkably efficient postal system, but censorship and a protective instinct generally resulted in carefully anodyne phrasing.

Wilfred, however, described his early experiences very clearly in letters that could leave Tom and Susan in no doubt about the ferocity of warfare, even in supposedly 'quiet' sectors. He spared his mother nothing and she would understand the effect on him. His usual jocular or elaborate phrasing vanished, and in short, dramatic but factual sentences he described his first encounter with enemy action: long hours of intense and suffocating darkness in a sunken dug-out ahead of the front line, tight-packed with soldiers under his command, pinned down by enemy shell-fire and unable to escape. With water rising steadily around them, there was little head-room, and the sentry posted on the steep steps was flung down and blinded by the blast of explosions at the entrance. It was during this ordeal that he kept calm by thinking of his family at home in Shrewsbury, going peacefully to church while he was in danger, trapped and helpless.

There was a brief time to recover and write home in his usual open-hearted style – but then came a different kind of torture in his second direct experience of action. He and his men spent two days and a night lying in the open, chilled beyond reason in the bitter cold of a wide unprotected hill-top. They could not move without being seen and shot at, buffeted by high explosives landing all around them. It felt like a frozen desert, abandoned and lifeless.

These were strongly contrasting episodes: one in heavy, underground darkness, the other in dazzling, hostile snow and frost; but both letters showed the intensity of the events and the extent of Wilfred's personal distress. Susan already knew well how much the sense of being trapped underground in complete darkness and danger would affect her son, in a kind of waking nightmare; and he had been equally trapped in the frozen field, lying motionless in the severe cold for many hours.

What she could not know was how these experiences would affect him in the ensuing months. 'The Sentry' was started in the summer of 1917 and developed in May 1918, while 'Exposure' was started in late 1917 and reflects the writer's sense of isolation in a cold and hostile landscape. In both poems there is the ultimately unbearable challenge and threat of front-line experience, set against Wilfred's boyhood pleasure in exploring landscape and the hills of south Shropshire. In one case he shows the inescapable noise and plunging blast of shell-fire on the dug-out and, in the other, the long hours of terrible silent danger endured in cold immobility in the open air. What at home had been happy exploration and understanding of the countryside became unbearable onslaughts on his mental state as he and his men clung to their self-control. Both poems are striking in their intense presentation of threat and horror, and 'Exposure' in particular shows how the poet could use his skills and feelings to depict the individual sense of danger:

> *Pale flakes with fingering stealth come feeling for our faces –*
> *We cringe in holes, back on forgotten dreams, and stare, snow-dazed,*
> *Deep into grassier ditches. So we drowse, sun-dozed,*
> *Littered with blossoms trickling where the blackbird fusses,*
> *Is it that we are dying?*

Both poems were completed in September 1918, and both demonstrate how Wilfred could use intense personal experience to show the universality of war, writing not directly about himself but expressing vividly what war could do.

Away behind the front line for a while, Wilfred rediscovered his usual jaunty tone in his letters, and wrote to his siblings as well as his mother. There are regular comments on Susan's ailments, together with assurances of his own good health despite the discomforts. He hoped to receive copies of *Punch* or, if possible, the latest *Poetry Review*. A steady stream of parcels from home brought personal items for washing and warmth, chocolate or biscuits, and magazines for idle moments. Above all, they brought reassurance and a sense of family love and solidarity.

The next brush with the hazards of war came in March, in a simple but somewhat ignominious incident: a fall of about 15 feet in the dark, into a cellar or well in a ruined house. Concussion meant a week in a Casualty Clearing Station, resting and watching barges on the Somme canal – but in early May he was back there again after another, more complex and significant encounter with enemy action.

In the early months of 1917 the front line had shifted noticeably to the east, as the Germans straightened their defences away from the old Somme front line (including the site of Wilfred's first encounter with the war in January) to the new fortified Hindenburg Line. In the British Army's attempts to break through it, the 2nd Manchesters were caught up in an attack on the city of Saint Quentin. On 14 April Wilfred led his troops round the outlying village of Fayet, and in the approach up a quiet valley there was time to pause and rest for a short while. Then, at the word of command, the men advanced with steady determination into the direct enemy fire that awaited them. Later, Wilfred described a kind of elation in this act of exposure, plunging directly into the barrage of gunfire, unprotected on the open hill-top.

This action emerged in one of Wilfred's last poems, 'Spring Offensive'. Again using his own direct experience to depict the truth of what war really felt like, his memory of home created the image of the gold of buttercups on the men's boots as they paused and rested – attention is turned away from himself and direct personal memory, on to the ordinary unnamed soldiers. He writes of the men's quiet advance uphill through, '... the long grass swirled / By the May breeze', and their halt before plunging out into danger ...

> *... they ponder the warm field*
> *And the far valley behind, where the buttercups*
> *Had blessed with gold their slow boots coming up;*
> *Where even the little brambles would not yield*
> *But clutched and clung to them like sorrowing arms ...*

They were all individuals who might dream of meadows in peacetime but had no escape from the reality of machine-gun fire aimed straight at them. These lines were later noted by Harold and linked to the memory of walking through the river meadows by the Severn, returning from evening service in Uffington church.

This challenging experience was followed by more than a week in the front line, digging trenches and reinforcements near Saint Quentin, often in rain and constantly under fire. The crisis for Wilfred came when a large shell explosion, close to where he was sleeping on a railway bank, left him half-buried for many hours. He awoke to the gruesome discovery of a dead friend who had been killed and buried there very recently, with the body now dismembered and scattered around him by the shell-blast. A week later, he was seen to be shaky, stammering and behaving oddly, and with his memory confused. Ironically for a man who placed such a high value on language and expression, he was clearly disturbed and unable to communicate.

Owen was sent to the familiar Casualty Clearing Station, which was now a specialist hospital for shell-shock cases. Here he spent three weeks resting from the front line – usually long enough for 'neurasthenic' patients to recover and return to active service. He did not tell Susan much about his condition, beyond indicating firmly that he was 'merely avoiding' a breakdown. He also asked her not to let anyone know that he was in hospital again. However, the poetry he wrote in later months reflected his state of mind. Shell-shock often brought a sense of suffocation, together with uncontrollable trembling, a rapid pulse and sweats, elements of boyhood nightmares accompanied by faces plunging at him in his dreams. In the middle of June he was sent back to England, first to Netley Hospital in Southampton and then to Craiglockhart, a new hospital for shell-shocked officers on the outskirts of Edinburgh.

To the world at large, this was all routine, part of the accumulating facts of modern warfare, and 1917 was hard for everyone. On the home front, although food was not yet rationed (this would come in 1918), food prices were rising and supplies were uncertain. For many households, with the main or only wage-earner absent and his return, or even survival, increasingly uncertain, women struggled to pay their rent and care for their children. Army allowances reached them but were barely adequate, and many women were taking up war work, or replacing men in factories or on buses and trams. It was also mostly the women who wrote and received letters by the million, and packed the steady stream of parcels for their soldier sons or brothers or lovers. Susan Owen cooked, saved and sent parcels 'assiduously', to use Harold's expression; small delicious or useful things which would travel well, such as chocolate, soap or socks – always needed – as well as toothpaste, hair oil or disinfectant. Special treats, such as whisky or cakes, would be sent too from many families, while the wealthier households would send hampers from big London stores.

By this time – the spring of 1917 – Harold had been obliged to give up the Royal Naval Air Service because he had exceeded the two crashes which were acceptable in training. When home on leave he must have seen the hangars being built at Monkmoor airfield, just up the road from home; but following his third crash he was told to look elsewhere, and joined the Royal Naval Reserve. In Shrewsbury, Tom Owen's work was vital to the war effort, since the railways were an essential part of military organisation, despite the departure of many of its workers to the army. He would contribute cigarettes for Susan's parcels, and towards the end of the war he composed an affectionate rhyme about the family which defined each member: Harold was '… a young man in the Navy …', Colin a '… nice boy in the Air Force …' and Mary, in the Red Cross, a young girl who '… did her bit …'. He himself was an '… old man of Shrewsbury …' and '… too

Fig. 64 *Monkmoor Airfield. By 1918 the busy airfield extended to both sides of Monkmoor Road and was used by the newly created Aerial Observation School. A few hangars survive in commercial or storage use or as car parks.*

old for the fray …'. Susan was '… a sweet lady …' whose only thought was to cheer their offspring in the years of '… horrible strife …'; while Wilfred was described as being slightly 'barmy' about poetry. Apart from the comment on Wilfred, Tom's lines could have been applied to almost any family in the country.

Wilfred Owen reached Craiglockhart Hospital on an overnight train towards the end of June 1917. A large breakfast in the North British Hotel came first, next to Waverley Station and the Scott Monument (reminders of Scott's novels, which Tom used to read to his family). Next, establishing himself fully in the city, Wilfred walked the length of Princes Street. He had been to Edinburgh once before: a tour of the sights had been an important feature of their family holiday with the Bulmans in 1912. Now, however, both Bill Bulman and Walter Forrest, Blanche Bulman's fiancé, were dead – the former killed at Gallipoli and the latter very recently at Gaza.

At Craiglockhart he found a large institution full of distressed and shell-shocked officers, with medical staff who had discovered an effective way to treat what later became known as Post Traumatic Stress Disorder (PTSD). The combination of this alarming medical condition and the first meeting between the two war poets, Sassoon and Owen, has become famous and much-dramatised, and is recognised as a significant literary encounter. In a letter to his mother on 15 August, 1917, he wrote to Susan:

Dearest Mother,

... I have just been reading Siegfried Sassoon, and am feeling at a very high pitch of emotion. Nothing like his trench life sketches has ever been written or ever will be written... That is why I have not yet dared to go up to him and parley in a casual way. He is here you know because he wrote a letter to the Higher Command which was too plain spoken. They promptly sent him over here!

In fact this moment – when Owen, the unknown and aspiring writer, approached Sassoon, the established and controversial poet – turned out to be the final essential element to the younger man's long and self-appointed apprenticeship. It was Sassoon, already much admired by Owen for his bold poetry and statement against the war, who encouraged Owen into his final flowering as a poet.

Sassoon was also the conduit into a more sophisticated literary world where Wilfred met poets, publishers and artists. Once the weeks in Craiglockhart had enabled him to emerge from his shell-shocked condition and regain his steadiness of mind, he was discharged to 'light duties' for about three months before several months of undramatic military routine in late 1917 and the first half of 1918. The first post meant managing the Officers' Mess in Scarborough, while the second brought the drudgery of training large cohorts of fresh conscripts in Ripon.

Compared with front line experiences and his momentous meeting with Sassoon, this was a time of mundane work, with the depressing duty of preparing young men for the front line. However, it provided Owen with time to think and write. In Scarborough he secured a quiet room for himself in the officers' mess, a hotel in peacetime, whose turret overlooking the sea was a perfect place to retreat in the evenings and write. In Wilfred's leisure time he worked at writing poetry or joined a fellow-officer to explore the town's antique shops and talk about literature: Philip Bainbrigge, who was extremely short-sighted and physically extremely ill-suited to military life, had enlisted in the Army on hearing of the death in action of two admired colleagues on the staff of Shrewsbury School. He was an entertaining and popular character with a talent for teaching the Classics, and quite apart from his teaching duties he would write witty and frequently obscene epigrams in Latin or Greek. By this time, Wilfred had gained enough experience of the world to be entertained by this sophistication and style, and he enjoyed Bainbrigge's intellect and humour.

In Ripon (his second posting) the military routine consisted of a grinding schedule of drilling and instructing the young men in army ways, but he also managed to rent an attic room in a local cottage. Here he could spend his time on writing steadily and with great concentration. The many drafts discovered after his death show how his ideas and language emerged at this time, and were refined into the poems that are read and studied a century after his death.

On New Year's Eve 1917 Wilfred wrote a reflective letter to his mother, looking back at episodes in his life and friendships, continuing:

> *... And so I have come to the true measure of man ... I go out of this year a Poet, my dear Mother, as which I did not enter it. I am held peer by the Georgians; I am a poet's poet ... But chiefly I thought of the very strange look on all faces in that camp* [Étaples]; *an incomprehensible look, which a man will never see in England ... It will never be painted, and no actor will ever seize it. And to describe it, I think I must go back and be with them.*

Among the significant elements that he identified were periods of labour, horrible danger – and, always: poetry, Susan's affection, and sympathy for the oppressed. He was also proud to claim his accepted status as a real poet, recognised by the leading writers of the day such as he had met through his friends Sassoon, Robert Graves and others. He also referred to the strange and 'incomprehensible' look, 'more terrible than terror', on the faces of men in the camp who were destined for the front line. He now recognised, six months after returning to England with shell-shock, that he must go back to help them.

Although he had seen some of his work appearing in the Craiglockhart house magazine, late in January 1918 he first saw the appearance of one of his poems in public print. The publication of 'Miners' in *The Nation* brought him his first earned fee and, justifiably, great pride. As a leading weekly journal of progressive news and opinion, *The Nation* was well-known to leading literary figures of the day, including H.G. Wells, the Sitwells and others, and one of the few periodicals willing to print criticism of the war. 'Miners' was written quickly, in instinctive response to news of

Fig. 65 (overleaf) *Shrewsbury railway lines photographed in November 1918. The main track to the east out of Shrewsbury Station, with the Hereford track branching off bottom right. Underdale Road runs across at the centre, with the white windows of Cleveland Place prominent. Monkmoor Road runs parallel beyond, with the broad open ground (top left) that lay opposite Mahim.*

a mining disaster with heavy loss of life. It reflects Wilfred's knowledge of geology, as the poem moves from coal burning in the domestic fireplace to its sources deep underground, and links the coal seams that were once prehistoric woodland with the desperate efforts of soldiers in Owen's war, struggling to dig tunnels and lay mines to explode and kill an unseen enemy. It ends:

> *The centuries will burn rich loads*
> *With which we groaned,*
> *Whose warmth shall lull their dreaming lids,*
> *While songs are crooned;*
> *But they will not dream of us poor lads,*
> *Left in the ground.*

The incidents in Wilfred's first months of active service were typical of this new kind of warfare, and seem to have affected him particularly badly. It is possible that the earlier concussion contributed to his state of mental confusion at this point – and it is a further irony, although beneficial on this occasion, that his shell-shock was severe enough for him to spend several crucial months away from the war. It gave him time, as he slowly recovered, to give expression to his true instincts and his voice as a writer.

In the spring of 1918 the country was in a desperate position in the face of the German Spring Offensive, designed to finish the war before American troops could swing the balance of manpower against them. It was for this purpose that the drill-sergeants and officers in the vast camp at Ripon were insistently training young conscripts as fast as possible, to reinforce the tired and over-stretched troops already on the ground. Some of what Wilfred saw here found its way into another poem, 'The Send-Off'. Written in Ripon in 1917, the poem has a universality in its depiction of a large, anonymous group of very young men. Hundreds of new conscripts received their basic training in this vast, bleak camp before being despatched in special train-loads to an unknown destination. Later there would be the returning few who '... May creep back, silent, to still village wells / Up half-known roads.' (The reference to 'still village wells' may relate to Dunsden, with its scattered rural houses and the important village well at its heart).

Wilfred was back in Scarborough when he was passed fit for active service. In August 1918 he had his final leave at home before returning to front-line service. It was a rushed visit, with Susan and Tom surely trying not to think about the prospects, let alone talk of them. All too many parents must have gone through the same experience, after nearly four years of war. The whole country knew that this was a critical moment and Wilfred, who knew that he must fulfil his determination to lead his men as best he could, was urgently organising his affairs. What to say, what to think; he told his mother of the bag of papers that must be burned – unread, unexamined – if he failed to return, and left in his desk the poems and drafts for which he could see a future. By this time he had assembled a list of work that he would submit for publication, and had begun to draft the Preface which subsequently became as widely known and influential as the best of his poetry.

Before crossing the Channel, there was time to meet Colin, who was based in Hastings with the RAF. Susan was there too, travelling faithfully by train for a last family farewell. In the vast military machine that the army had begun, Wilfred first spent a week at Étaples, where he discussed anthologies of war poetry and other non-military topics with Conal O'Riordan, an Irish novelist and playwright, and a former director of the Abbey Theatre in Dublin. He was described by Wilfred as '... an extraordinary hunch-backed little Irishman', who ran the YMCA Rest Hut at the Base Camp in Étaples during the First World War. In terms that would have delighted Susan Owen, O'Riordan later recalled that there could have been 'no cheerier companion or blither soul than charming young Wilfred Owen'. They talked constantly about books, life and people, until Wilfred was posted to spend a week in Amiens, with time to explore and muse at the half-empty and war-damaged city. He asked Susan, back in Shrewsbury, to tell Harold and Colin (but only them) how pleased he was to be back at the war and well away from everything that was typical of conventional English everyday life.

By mid-September he was back with the 2nd Manchesters as part of the Fourth Army, and there was time to work on a few poems and send some to Sassoon. He heard from home that Harold had joined the light cruiser HMS *Astraea* off the coast of South Africa. Then the Manchesters moved eastwards, until they were close to the area round Saint Quentin where Wilfred had been in action over a year before. By now the large-scale German advance in the spring had been turned and the British Army was steadily advancing again. Tactics had changed, and it was recognised that many German units were losing heart. There was a sense of coming towards the end of the war.

Letters back to Shrewsbury continued to specify what he would like to receive in parcels from home, in the way of chocolate bars and small personal items. He also confided in Susan about being close to enemy bombardment, but with the reassurance that there was nothing as bad as his first experiences in 1917. He reported the death of friends – including Philip Bainbrigge, the Shrewsbury schoolmaster whose company he had enjoyed in Scarborough – and the disgust of another young officer, just back from leave in London, at the indifference he saw there to the real meaning of the war.

The British army was now making deep inroads into the large area of Northern France which had suffered under German occupation throughout the war, and on 1 October Wilfred successfully led his men in a small but fierce engagement. This was

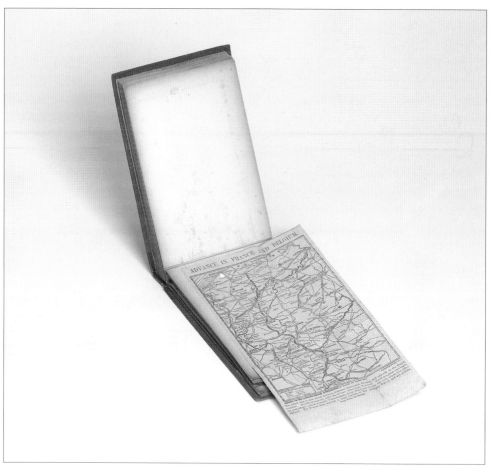

Fig. 66 *Tom's notebook with front line map showing the final advancing stages of the British Army in 1918.*

in Joncourt, a village a few miles north of Saint Quentin where he had been driven into the disabling state of shell-shock; but this time his hard-won settled emotions served him well, enabling him to deal with intense enemy action. He captured and held a front-line enemy machine-gun post, in what he described in his letter to Susan a few days later as 'SHEER' fighting. Above all, he was able to bring her the good news that his nerves were in perfect order. He repeated this phrase to Sassoon too, but admitted to him that his senses were deadened and that he would 'feel again' as soon as he dared – but not yet, as he dealt with the administrative aftermath of battle, writing 'Deceased' on personal letters to the families of fallen comrades. His poem 'Insensibility' was written long before this, but it describes and reflects on the self-protective insensitivity that he had observed in the army.

Wilfred also told his mother that his action and leadership had brought a recommendation for the Military Cross (in the event this was confirmed after his death).

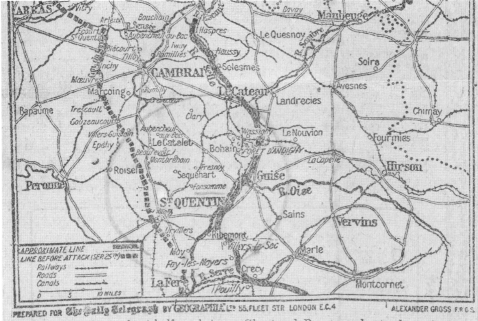

The allied line is now about halfway between Ghent and Bruges, and extends to the Dutch frontier. British troops are only about two miles from Tournai. Good progress was made in yesterday's attack towards Valenciennes, from which our forces are now about five miles distant. The French have cleared a large portion of the Andigny Forest and are getting very close to Guise.

Fig. 67 *Detail of Fig. 68 (opposite), showing the area north of St Quentin where Wilfred won his Military Cross and where he was killed a month later (1918).*

The citation, from the Artists' Rifles Roll of Honour, reads:

> *2nd Lt. Owen, WS*
> *Fonsomme Line: For conspicuous gallantry and devotion to duty in the attack. On the company commander becoming a casualty, he assumed command and showed fine leadership, and resisted a heavy counter attack. He personally manipulated a captured enemy machine gun from an isolated position, and inflicted considerable losses on the enemy. Throughout he behaved most gallantly.*

A period of rest came next for his whole battalion – although, as he complained lightly to his cousin Leslie Gunston, military 'rest' always meant constant duties. However, there was time for letters home, thanking for parcels, including *Punch* and asking for the next *New Statesman*, before the unit rejoined the front line. Wilfred wrote next about being billeted in a French household in Bohain, newly liberated by British troops, where the half-starved population was bewildered and delighted

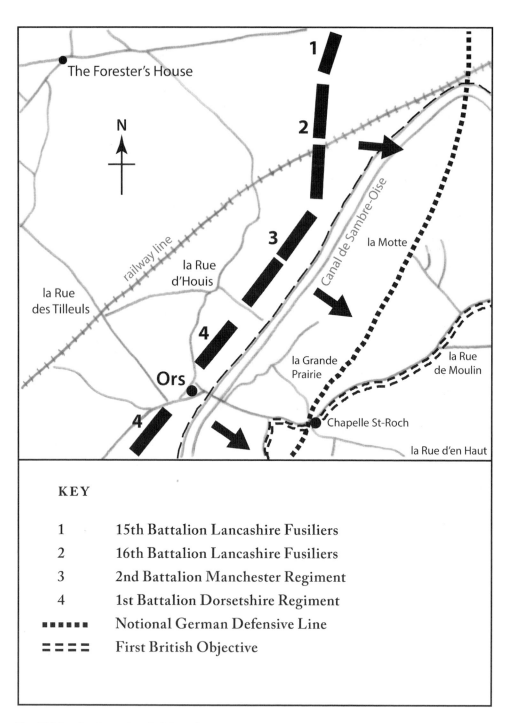

The Forester's House

N

1

2

la Motte

3

la Rue
d'Houis

la Rue
des Tilleuls

railway line

Canal de Sambre-Oise

4

la Grande
Prairie

la Rue
de Moulin

Ors

4

Chapelle St-Roch

la Rue d'en Haut

KEY

1	15th Battalion Lancashire Fusiliers
2	16th Battalion Lancashire Fusiliers
3	2nd Battalion Manchester Regiment
4	1st Battalion Dorsetshire Regiment
▪▪▪▪▪▪	Notional German Defensive Line
====	First British Objective

Fig. 68 *Map showing action of 4 November 1918.*

at their freedom after four years of harsh occupation and isolation. Wilfred's fluent knowledge of French and previous employment in the country made him a fine visitor as the British Army forced the enemy slowly back towards the frontier, and there is a touching sense in his letter of his pleasure at being able to show off his linguistic skill and appreciation of his hosts' heartfelt welcome.

The Manchesters moved forward again, and this time they knew that their target was a major onslaught on the Sambre-Oise canal, some 25 miles north-east of Saint Quentin. Most modern visitors to the old Western Front in northern France see broad open fields of arable crops, but if they go to Ors, with its bridge and lock on the broad working canal, the landscape can easily remind them of traditional, rural England: small fields, cattle, copses, farms and woodlands. For Owen, who had grown up constantly aware of first the Mersey and then the Severn, it was a small coincidence to find himself in such surroundings, and he would have felt at home with the local inhabitants – from one waterway to another; from a provincial centre in rural England to a small village in rural France. The canal was an important trade link for the region's great industrial production to the north, with a major railway line nearby. Railways, waterways, steel rail tracks and river banks, with the working countryside never far away: elements that were very familiar in Shrewsbury, part of the ordinary background to daily life and leisure.

The Sambre-Oise canal, which runs through the village of Ors, was the last natural obstacle to be overcome, and success here would be a significant contribution to the end of the war. A major assault was in preparation along several miles of the canal bank. All the bridges had been blown up or otherwise destroyed. The enemy forces were well dug in along the opposite banks and it would clearly be a hard-fought engagement.

In Ors, these were already difficult times. Many of the population were suffering from the Spanish Flu epidemic. Horses and farm carts had been requisitioned by the occupying German forces, and the sick had to lie on hay in the stables. In one family farm in the village, Marie Polvent had recovered from the flu and was trying to organise evacuation for her sick family. The Red Cross could not help, but a mule cart was located to transport Marie's elderly mother, and they moved to a small local hamlet. During the second half of October the village emptied slowly. Although food was difficult for the villagers, some milk and meat was provided from cows hidden from the occupying German forces. It is unlikely that Lieutenant Wilfred Owen met any of the local residents as the preparations continued for the battle. The first task of the British troops was to assemble and install several temporary bridges for the main forces. The senior officers in charge of the operation were worried at the situation on this particular stretch of the assault, since the attack to cross the canal here would be overlooked by German machine-guns at quite close quarters on the far side of the water.

On 31 October, Wilfred wrote to his mother once more, from what he called 'The Smoky Cellar of the Forester's House', in the woodland just outside Ors. It was a warm, loving and reassuring message, speaking of his own concern for her – above all, emphasising the rightness of his place at that moment, and the strength of companionship that surrounded him in their cramped quarters. It ended with an assurance that the danger would be long over by the time his letter reached her:

> *… I hope that you are as warm as I am; as serene in your room as I am here; and that you think of me never in bed as resignedly as I think of you always in bed – of this I am certain you could not be visited by a band of friends half so fine as surround me here. Ever Wilfred*

The letter went on its way like its many predecessors, slowly but reliably in the British forces' postal system, back to Shrewsbury and its tranquil setting on the River Severn. The date when it reached Mahim is not known, but it was probably on or very soon after the assault on the canal at Ors. In the first days of November there were brisk encounters with the enemy forces, in the struggle to clear them from the British side of the canal. The assault to cross the canal began early on 4 November almost before dawn, and the Manchesters' part in it was over by mid-morning. The troops lined up in the darkness. The first sections of the temporary bridge were assembled under protective covering fire, but very quickly the teams of soldiers constructing the bridge came under heavy enemy fire as they worked on the canal bank or on the open water.

Lieutenant Wilfred Owen and his men came under heavy machine-gun fire as they worked on the bridge. His body was identified later in the day, shot through the head, either at the edge of the water or out on a raft, in full view as he directed operations. He was buried in the communal cemetery in Ors three days later, alongside other victims of the battle. Two officers in the 2nd Manchesters were posthumously awarded the Victoria Cross: 2nd Lieutenant James Kirk, who paddled a raft out into the canal with a machine gun under heavy fire, and continued firing until he was killed; and Major Marshall, similarly killed while exposed to direct fire as he tried to cross the canal. Earlier, in September, Wilfred had described the latter as:

> *'Major Marshall of the ten wounds is the most arrant utterly soldierly soldier I ever came across … Bold, robust, dashing, unscrupulous, cruel, jovial, immoral, vast-chested, handsome-headed, of free, coarse speech …'*

Fig. 69 (right) *Tom's scrapbook: a newspaper cutting showing the Roll of Honour containing Wilfred's death. Tom has annotated the cutting with his son's Military Cross and the Victoria Cross won by a fellow officer. The two men are buried in the same military cemetery. The second 'killed in action' cutting gives the family's home address in Shrewsbury.*

ROLL OF HONOUR.

171 CASUALTIES TO OFFICERS.

64 REPORTED DEAD.

THE ARMY.

The following casualties are announced by the War Office :—

KILLED.

ANDERSON, Sec. Lt., A. D., G. Gds.
BAXTER, Sec. Lt., J. D. P., Lond. R.
CHISHOLM, Maj. E. A., M.C., R.F.A.
DODD, Sec. Lt. J. O'C., R. Muns. Fus.
ESDAILE, Capt. A. J., Devon R.
FRYER, Sec. Lt. C. J. G., M.C., Herts R.
HUDSPITH, Lt. W. L., Midd'x R.
HUNKIN, Lt. W. B. C., R. Welsh Fus.
JONES-BATEMAN, Capt. F., R. Welsh Fus.
VC KIRK, Sec. Lt. J., Manch. R.
LEONARD, Sec. Lt. D., M.M., Yorks R.

LLEWELLYN, Sec. Lt. V. R. Welsh Fus.
MACINTYRE, Sec. Lt. C. F. D., R.F.A.
OWEN, Capt. M. de B., Herts R.
OWEN, Sec. Lt. W. E. S., Manch. R. **M.C.**
PADLEY, Sec. Lt. P., R.F.A.
POWELL, Sec. Lt. W. E. G. P. W., W. Gds.
ROBINSON, Maj. F. A., M.C., Tank Corps
SHAW, Lt. W. D., R. Fus., att. Manch. R.
TROTMAN, Sec. Lt. F. H. L., Devon R.
TRYON, Maj. G. A., M.C., K.R. Rif. C.
VINCENT, Lt. A. E., R.F.A.

Previously reptd. Missing, believed Killed, now reptd. Killed.
SMITH, Sec. Lt. A. W., M.C., Gord. Highrs.

Previously reptd. Missing, now reptd. Killed.
RENNIE, Sec. Lt. A., R. Scots
CURRIE, Sec. Lt. W. G., M.C., Linc. R.
MANGER, Sec. Lt. E., M.G.C.
SMITH, Sec. Lt. T., R. Scots

DIED OF WOUNDS.

BLENKINSOP, Lt. W. M., Durh. L.I.
BLYTH, Lt. W., M.G.C.
BROCK, Lt. C. H., Devon R.
CLAPHAM, Lt. E., D. of Well. R.
EVANS, Sec. Lt. N. E., R.F.A.
FORD, Sec. Lt. D. M., Sco. Rif.
WESTCOTT, Capt. E., M.C., W. Yorks R.

Previously reptd. Wounded, now reptd. Died of Wounds.
DRAPER, Sec. Lt. J., L.N. Lan. R.
MEWSON, Sec. Lt. FitzA. R. R.F.A.

DIED.

ANDERSON, Maj. G. G., R.A.M.C.
BROAD, Maj. R. B., R.F.A.
CLEE, Lt. T. H., Worc. R., att. Lan. Fus.
HICKEY, Sec. Lt. D., Leins. R.
MEADOWCROFT, Sec. Lt. J., R.E.
PEARSON, Capt. J. S., A.S.C. att. R.G.A.
PETTIGREW, Lt. John, Spec. List. att. S. Persia Rif.
RICHARDSON, Capt. P. B., M.G.C.
SCHUH, Capt. R. O., M.C., Devon R.
WALLS, Sec. Lt. F. N., A.S.C.
WILEY, Lt. E. O. S., Durh. L.I.
WILFORD, Lt. L. R., S. Staff. R.

KILLED IN ACTION.

OWEN.—Killed in action, on the 4th Nov., 1918, in France, SEC. LIEUT. WILFRED E. S. OWEN, 5th Batt. Manchester Regiment, eldest son of Mr. and Mrs. Tom Owen, Mahim, Monkmoor-road, Shrewsbury, aged 25 years.

Today the standard white British headstones of these two men are among the 59 graves, including Wilfred Owen's, in their clearly-defined section within the communal cemetery in Ors. Others who were killed in the same assault are in a separate cemetery closer to the canal.

Overall, the attack on a long stretch of the canal was a success and troops crossed over at several points on temporary bridges. It was the final major assault of the war, and a week later the Armistice came into effect.

The young British officer, for whom two years of independence in Bordeaux and the Pyrenees had been the equivalent of a university, and who was deeply influenced by French language and literature, would have enjoyed the company of the people in Ors and recognised their way of life. In the end, it seems, Wilfred's years of growing up in Shrewsbury alongside the River Severn were oddly echoed in his death, aged only 25, by a different waterway in the country which he had come to feel as his second home.

Aftermath

WHEN Wilfred Owen was killed, he was barely known as a poet and his reputation grew slowly in the decades after his death. Despite her intense grief, Susan followed his instructions and burned his bag of papers unread. The first publication of his poems came in 1920, the combined work of Siegfried Sassoon as his first friend in English literature and Edith Sitwell who had also known him. Next came another war poet, Edmund Blunden, who never met Wilfred but who fought throughout the war, became a friend of Sassoon and Robert Graves and whose poetry was profoundly in sympathy with Owen's approach and style. He produced a fuller edition of the poems in 1931, together with a biographical sketch. In wider circles, Wilfred remained little known or was viewed as 'bad for morale' because of the strength and clarity of his descriptions of the effects of the war. His work was sometimes seen as questioning the sacrifices that led to victory in 1918, expressing unhelpful 'softness' or, worse, reluctance to fight.

The approaching shadow of another world war and growing anxieties about the political and military threats of the 1930s meant that Owen's depiction of what war meant in human terms was scorned or disregarded. He continued to find readers and admirers, however, and as attitudes and political understanding changed in the years after the Second World War his writing gradually moved towards its present place in English literature.

A fresh impetus came in the 1960s, with the fiftieth anniversary of the 1918 armistice. Along with new writing that reflected the Second World War, often in relation to the preceding conflict, Benjamin Britten's 'War Requiem' in 1962 brought a new audience, combining Owen's poetry with the traditional requiem mass. Harold's three volumes of memoirs, *Journey from Obscurity*, were published in 1963–65 and give a striking picture of the pattern of life for the Owens, with all their aims and travails and their personalities. The subsequent appearance of Wilfred's *Collected Letters* in 1967 brought

Fig. 70 (left) *The original wooden cross on Wilfred Owen's grave in Ors, photographed in the 1920s by John Foulkes, who fought alongside him on the canal bank at Ors.*

his vivid correspondence and personality directly into the public gaze; showing his developing character bringing his poetry into even sharper focus for a later generation. By the time of the centenary of the First World War, Wilfred Owen was one of its best-known voices, and his poetry was widely taught and translated into other languages: his views on warfare and human suffering had found a universal audience.

One of the most frequently used comments on modern warfare was written in the spring of 1918. As Wilfred Owen was preparing poems for publication he drafted the Preface. It expressed his attitude to the war and his own purpose in writing about it – and although he did not see it printed in his lifetime it has become a source of frequent quotation and comment on war, as much as his most famous poems. It has provided titles for books and at least one well-known play, and is quoted frequently by journalists at many levels and by modern soldiers and poets:

> *This book is not about heroes. English poetry is not yet fit to speak of them.*
> *Nor is it about deeds, or lands, nor anything about glory, honour, might,*
> *majesty, dominion, or power, except War.*
> *Above all I am not concerned with Poetry.*
> *My subject is War, and the pity of War.*
> *The Poetry is in the pity.*
> *Yet these elegies are to this generation in no sense consolatory. They may be to*
> *the next. All a poet can do today is warn. That is why the true Poets must be*
> *truthful.*

Tom and Susan Owen came to Shrewsbury with a history of different trades, crafts and places in their families. Tom's mother had a Wiltshire background but married a Nantwich man, and work brought them to Shrewsbury before Tom knew the town. Susan's parents were both Oswestry people, but one of her sisters married a London doctor originally from Ireland, and the husband of her other sister, Emma, was a Londoner who later lived near Reading. When Tom was a young man he lodged with his parents in Shrewsbury, but as a railway employee he might have found work almost anywhere in the country.

For those few years of family life from 1907, Shrewsbury was the place which shaped the life of Tom and Susan's adolescent children; and the ancient town, the river, the Roman site at Uriconium, the schools and the fine countryside were all part of their young lives.

Wilfred's death in 1918 marked the end of close family life. Harold left the Navy, failed to achieve a professional career as an artist, but eventually married and settled happily to live near Dunsden, where he continued to paint. Mary never left home and did not live independently until both her parents had died – Tom in 1931 and Susan

Fig. 71 *The Owen family without Wilfred. Colin aged 17, Harold 20 and Mary 21. They are dressed formally, perhaps for a special occasion as Tom has a cigar (1917).*

in 1942. Mary died in 1956. Colin, who always loved outdoor life and riding, worked on a farm at Cressage, in Shropshire, until he was old enough to join in the war. His post-war career took him into the Probation Service and he settled in Kenya, where he became the country's senior probation officer.

In the end, therefore, the whole family moved on from 1918. When the Armistice ended the fighting, Wilfred was dead and lay in France, the country that he had come to love and see as his second home; Harold was a rare visitor on leave from the Navy, and Colin was in the RAF. Tom never reached the post of Superintendent at Shrewsbury Station, with the better salary that it would have provided. He, Susan and Mary continued to live in Mahim until his retirement in 1925, and after a short interval in Somerset they settled in Emmer Green, near Reading, where they named their house 'Wilmot'. This brought them close to the family support of the Gunstons – and to Dunsden, where Wilfred had spent two difficult but formative years in his adolescence. Tom, Susan, Mary and Harold are all buried in Dunsden churchyard, as is the Revd Herbert Wigan, Wilfred's old mentor in the village.

A hundred years on, Wilfred Owen's name can be seen on war memorial tablets in St Julian's church and Shrewsbury Abbey, as well as in Westminster Abbey and

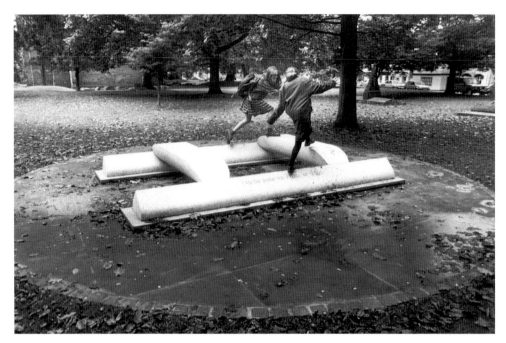

Fig. 72 *'Symmetry', the memorial created by Paul de Monchaux, inaugurated in 1993 to mark the centenary of Wilfred's birth. The line, 'I am the enemy you killed my friend' comes from the poem 'Strange Meeting'.*

Manchester Cathedral. Birkenhead remembers the family's years there and Edinburgh has not forgotten his stay at Craiglockhart, now part of a large university campus with rooms named after Wilfred Owen and Siegfried Sassoon. There are plaques in his memory on Mahim, the household of his crucial later adolescent years, and on the cottage in Ripon where much of his most enduring poetry was written. Not far from Monkmoor Road, Shrewsbury now has the Wilfred Owen junior school, which has links with the village school in Ors, close to the British military graves in the communal cemetery. In 1993, the centenary of his birth, the Wilfred Owen Association commissioned the memorial 'Symmetry', in the grounds of Shrewsbury Abbey; and Ors remembers him with a ceremony on 4 November every year, to commemorate his part in the liberation of the village from its years of occupation during the First World War.

Shrewsbury continued calmly on its own way after 1918. The river was tamed to some extent, with flood defences limiting the regular damage and alarm. Population, housing and employment numbers grew steadily, particularly after the Second World War. The railways – the reason for Tom Owen's presence in the town – occupy less freight-handling space, but still connect the town efficiently with the outside world, and the station retains its fine nineteenth-century buildings. Some buildings in the town remain from Monkmoor Airfield, and although they are used as sales premises or for storage, they are still recognisable as survivors from the First World War.

In the twenty-first century it would take some effort for Tom and Susan to recognise their part of Shrewsbury. Although No. 1 Cleveland Place and Mahim are still visibly unchanged from the Owens' time, the residential suburbs around the Abbey, in Underdale, Cherry Orchard and Abbey Foregate, have grown outwards to the north and east, including the old racecourse, which was used as an airfield after the First World War and then for fresh wartime service buildings in the Second World War. The ground to the south of the Abbey still has traces of the old light railway alongside a large car-park, but the site of the prisoner-of-war camp and the old Carriage Works is now taken up with a supermarket and commercial buildings.

Apart from the great growth in housing estates, the style and status of the whole area was greatly changed with the introduction of the new road bridge over the Severn between Monkmoor on one side and the big light industrial and commercial areas of Ditherington and Harlescott on the other. Underdale and Monkmoor, the quiet roads that led only to the river banks or the Uffington ferry, are now busy routes for the constant flow of traffic from one part of the town to another, or on to the outside world.

There is no longer a ferry across the River Severn to Uffington.

Partial family tree for the Owens and the Shaws (with key figures, including cousins, shown in bold).

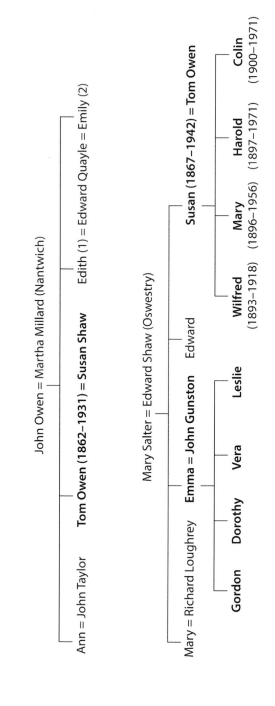

Roundel

In Shrewsbury Town e'en Hercules wox tired,
  Tired of the streets that end not up nor down;
  Tired of the Quarry, though seats may be hired
          Of Shrewsbury Town.

  Tired of the tongues that knew not his renown;
  Tired of the Quarry Bye-Laws, so admired
  By the Salopian, the somnambulant clown.

  Weak as a babe, and in like wise attired,
  He leaned upon his club; frowned a last frown,
  And of ineffable boredom, so expired
          In Shrewsbury Town.

Wilfred Owen

Select Bibliography

Of the many books on Wilfred Owen's life and writing, and the sources of his inspiration, I have made extensive use of *Wilfred Owen – Collected Letters* (ed. Harold Owen and John Bell, OUP, 1974) and *The Poems of Wilfred Owen* (ed. Jon Stallworthy, Chatto & Windus, 1990). Other material on Owen has been drawn from the full biographies by Jon Stallworthy (OUP, 1974), Dominic Hibberd (Weidenfeld & Nicholson, 2003) and Guy Cuthbertson (Yale, 2015); from two further works by Dominic Hibberd: *Owen the Poet* (Palgrave Macmillan, 1989) and *Wilfred Owen – the Last Year 1917–1918* (Constable, 1993); and from Jane Potter: *Wilfred Owen: An Illustrated Life* (Bodleian Library Publishing, 2014). Other significant writers on Owen have included: Edmund Blunden, C. Day Lewis, D.S. Welland, Douglas Kerr and Merryn Williams. Although now out of print, also of considerable interest is *Anthem for a Doomed Youth* (The Woburn Press, 1987) by Kenneth Simcox, a local Shrewsbury author and retired teacher.

Fig. 73 *Monogram cast from a graphic design by Wilfred Edward Salter Owen, first used to sign off a letter in 1907, and now used by the Wilfred Owen Association as its logo.*

Harold Owen's memoirs provide a rich picture of the Owen family and their lives. In the light of his older brother's posthumous fame, Harold gave Wilfred considerable attention, particularly in the first volume of the memoirs: Harold Owen, *Memoirs of the Owen Family, Journey from Obscurity, I: Childhood* (OUP, 1963); *II: Youth* (OUP, 1964); *III: War* (OUP, 1965).

Further information on the life and work of Wilfred Owen is provided by the Wilfred Owen Association, set up in 1989: www.wilfredowen.org.uk.

I learned a great deal about the patterns of Shrewsbury's history and development from Barrie Trinder's *Beyond the Bridges* (Phillimore, 2006). The digital reference material available through Shropshire Archives (www.shropshirearchives.org.uk) provided an essential and invaluable source of material on the town's history and growth.

IMAGE CREDITS

Images from the Wilfred Owen Archive copyright © Bodleian Library, University of Oxford, reproduced with kind permission of the Trustees of the Wilfred Owen Estate: **Fig. 1**, Box 26, 1A e; **Fig. 2**, Box 32, item 22; **Fig. 3**, Box 36, 2b a; **Fig. 4**, Box 36, 2B b; **Fig. 7**, Box 28, Book 4; **Fig. 26**, Box 36, 1B a; **Fig. 31**, Box 34, 4A d; **Fig. 46**, Box 34, 4B a; **Fig. 47**, Box 36, 2C b; **Fig. 49**, f2e(c)1; **Fig. 53**, Box 35, 8I/J I; **Fig. 54**, Box 36, 2D a; **Fig. 55**, Box 36, 2D e; **Fig. 62**, Box 34, 4A e; **Figs. 66 & 67**, Box 28; **Fig. 69**, Box 28; **Fig. 70**, Box 28; **Fig. 71**, f.2e(c).

Images reproduced with kind permission of Shropshire Archives. Copyright © Shropshire Archives with additional copyright stated where relevant: **Page ii**, PH/S/13/F/2/6; **Fig. 8**, PH/S/13/S/34/15; **Fig. 9**, (swimmers) PH/S/13/Q/2/96; **Fig. 10**, (baths) PH/S/13/Q/2/92; **Fig. 12**, PH/S/13/5/22/192; **Fig. 13**, PH/S/13/A/5/68; **Fig. 14** (J. Mallinson), PH/S/13/S/22/194; **Fig. 15**, PH/S/13/A/1/21; **Fig. 16**, PH/S/13/C/21/22; **Fig. 17**, PH/S/13/Q/2/8; **Fig. 18**, PH/S/13/T/2/3; **Fig. 19** (Mallinson), PH/S/13/F/2/121; **Fig. 20**, PH/S/13/A/6/19; **Fig. 21 & cover** (Frith), PH/S/13/E/1/80; **Fig. 22**, PH/S/13/A/5/265; **Fig. 23**, PH/S/13/A/5/25; **Fig. 24**, PH/S/13/A/5/12; **Fig. 25**, PH/S/13/A/5/13; **Fig. 27**, PH/S/13/M/13/34; **Fig. 28** (Frith), PH/S/13/S/9/5; **Fig. 29**, PH/S/13/R/3/17; **Fig. 30**, PH/S/13/A/1/86; **Fig. 32**, PH/S/13/C/5/25; **Fig. 34** © West Midland Photo Services Ltd., PH/S/13/M/2/21; **Fig. 35**, PH/S/13/M/6/58; **Fig. 36** © V. Bryant, PH/S/13/C/2/21; **Fig. 37**, PH/U/1/46; **Fig. 38**, PH/U/1/35; **Fig. 39** (Mallison), PH/U/1/39; **Fig. 40**, PH/S/13/P/2/38; **Fig. 41**, PH/S/13/S/22/159; **Fig. 42**, PH/S/13/W/7/28; **Fig. 43** from painting by T. Prytherch, PH/W/38/3/13; **Fig. 44**, PH/S/13/C/5/24; **Fig. 48**, PH/S/13/A/5/325; **Fig. 50**, PH/S/13/S/28/15; **Fig. 51**, PH/S/13/M/13/25; **Fig. 52**, PH/S/13/M/13/18/1; **Fig. 56**, PH/S/13/B/2/54; **Fig. 57**, PH/S/13/A/5/354; **Fig. 58**, PH/S/13/C/21/28; **Fig. 61**, PH/S/13/S/22/89; **Fig. 63** (W.J. 'Jack' Slack), PH/S/14/1/93; **Fig. 64**, PH/S/13/M/13/22; **Fig. 65**, PH/S/13/M/13/23.

Other images are copyrighted as follows: **Fig. 5**, photographer unknown; **Fig. 6, Fig. 33** and **Fig. 45** © Elizabeth Owen; **Fig. 11** © Gordon Dickins; **Fig. 59** (civilian) DSW/1/1/4/5/4 and **Fig. 60** (uniform) DSW/1/1/4/5/2 © The John Rylands Library, The University of Manchester by kind permission of the Wilfred Owen Estate; **Fig. 68** © Richard Wheeler; **Fig. 72** © Liz Kessler; **Fig. 73** © John Dangerfield; **Fig. 74** © Denis May.

Index

Abbey Foregate Literary Society 7
Artists Rifles 95, 98, 99, 115
Bagnères de Bigorre 82, *86*
Bainbrigge, Philip 108, 109, 113
Birkenhead 5–7, 9, 21, 41, 53
    Institute 5, *7*, 10, 34, 35, 88
    Public baths 14
Bordeaux 79, 80, 90, 93, 95, 99, 120
    University 82
British Army 94, 99, 105, 113, *114*, 117
Bulman, Nellie 69
Carline's House 25, *37*
Craiglockhart Hospital 107
Dunsden 63, 66–74, *69*, *71*, 76, 88, 112,
    122, 123
Geology 28, 39, 58, 62, 112
Gunston family 8, 48, 54, 65, 66, 70, 123
    Emma 8, 20, 47
    John 48, 95, 99
    Leslie *47*, 79, 115
Haughmond Hill 15, 52, 54, *59*
Hazledine, William 23, *24*, 32, 87
Joncourt 114
Keats 58, 64, 66, 68, 74
King George V 51, 53, 82, *83*
Léger family 82, *86*, 86–88, 90, 93
Mahim *x*, *42*, *51*, 52, 124, 125
Matriculation 38, 59, 65, 66, 77
Ors *116*, 116–118, *120*, 124
Oswestry 5–9, *8*, 21, 47, *72*, 76, 102, 122
Owen family
    Colin *2*, 5, 9, 11, 22, 34, 54, 56, *72*, 74, 81, 83,
      87, 90, *102*, 107, 113, *123*
    Harold *2*, 3, 5, 9, 11, 15–17, 21, 28, 33–35, 39,
      41, 44, 45, 48, 52, 54, 56, 65, 68, 70, *72*,

73, 76, *78*, 81, 83, 87, 90, 102, 106, 107,
    113, 122, *123*
    Memoirs: *Journey from Obscurity* 1, 6, 9,
      35, 44, 49, 51, 56, 59, 65, 76, 121
    Mary *2*, 5, 9, 11, 15, 21, 34, 47, 53, 68, 74, 76,
      82, 83, 90, 102, 107, 122, *123*
    Susan 1, *2*, 5-9, 11, 14, 17, 20, 21, 34–36, 41,
      42, 44–48, 51–54, 57, 66–68, *72*, 72–74, 76,
      77, 80, 81, 87, 90, 94, 99, 102–109, 112-114,
      121–123, *123*
    Tom *2*, 5–7, 9, 14–17, 21, 27, 34, 36, 41, 42,
      44–47, 51–54, 64, *72*, 74–76, 79, 80, 82, 84,
      90, 99, 102, 103, 107, 112, *114*, *119*,
      122, *123*
    Wilfred Owen Collected Letters 121, 128
    Wilfred Owen Memorials 123, *124*
    Wilfred Owen Preface 113, 122
Plas Wilmot *2*, 7–9, *8*, 17
Poems
    'Deep under turfy grass' 70
    'Exposure' 104
    'Insensibility' 114
    'Miners' 62, 109
    'Roundel' 127
    'Spring Offensive' 56, 105
    'The Sentry' 44, 104
Poetry Bookshop 100
Ragge, Mary 22, 42, 53, 54, 57, 83
Reading 8, 66, 74, 98, 123
    University 73, 77, 79, 80, 82
Railways *ix*, *x*, 3, 4, 5, 6, 7, 9, 33, *39*, 53, 74, *85*,
    92, *110*, 117, 124
    Accident *45*
    Shrewsbury Station 6, *12*, 29, *39*
    Light Railway 25, 33, 75, *77*, 125

Fig. 74 (left) *'The Letter' by Denis May (b.1929). A mother and child safe at home compose a letter in the midst of their dreams and fears, and images of soldiers at war – an experience shared by millions of households between 1914 and 1918. This linocut is one of a series of 70 prints inspired by Owen's war poems, and created between 1962 and 1989. As an art student in the late 1940s Denis May learned about the realities of war from tutors fresh from war service. He became a Lecturer in Art Education and Director of Teacher Training and Education at Portsmouth Polytechnic, and his response to Owen's poetry was intensified by his own father's experience of the First World War and the strength of their shared reaction to Benjamin Britten's War Requiem, with its inclusion of four of Owen's poems.*

Religion
  Bible study 8, 39, 41, 44
  Congregationalist 37, 38
  Faith 36, 38, 39, 46, 54, 68–70, 73, 74
  Keswick Convention 41, 70
  United Reformed Church *vii*, *viii*, 37, 38, *39*
  Ripon 108, 109, 112, 124
Sambre-Oise Canal *116*, 117
Sassoon, Siegfried 108, 109, 113, 114, 121, 124
Scarborough 7, 17, 54, 108, 112, 113
Schools
  Berlitz School, Bordeaux 80, 82, 93
  Birkenhead Institute 5, *7*, 10, 34, 35, 88
  Shrewsbury Borough Technical School *37*, 95
  Pupil-Teacher Centre 38, 60, 65
  Wyle Cop School *viii*, 58, *62*, 102
Severn, River 3, 4, 14, 18, 23, *24*, 29, 61, 117, 120, 125
Shaw Jnr, Edward 8, 76, 126
Shaw Snr, Edward 7, 9, 126
Shrewsbury
  Abbey Foregate *x*, 25, 27, 32, 33, 37, *39*, 42, 61, 75
  Belle Vue *91*,
  Canon Street 9
  Cherry Orchard *x*, 4, 9, 15, 125
  Cleveland Place *x*, *15*, 16, 34, 51, *110*, 125
  English Bridge *viii*, 6, 14, 19, 22, 29, *30*, *32*, 37, *39*, 75
  Library 49, 64
  Longden Coleham 22, 23, *24*, 37, *95*
  Monkmoor Road *x*, 15, 17, 19, 22, *42*, *51*, 52, 54, 83, 87, 107, *110*, 124, 125
  Museum *viii*, 49, 53, 61, 62, *64*
  Prisoner-of-war Camp *x*, 26, *92*, 125
  Shrewsbury Abbey vii, *x*, 15, *19*, 20, 22–26, *23*, 32, *39*, 41, 42, *46*, 57, 75, *77*, 92, 123, 124
  St Alkmund's Church *viii*, 17, *30*, 37
  St Julian's Church *viii*, 17, *30*, 42, *43*, 44, 123
  Underdale Road and ferry *x*, 6, 15, *16*, 17, 21, 22, 38, 56, *110*, 125
  United Reformed Church *vii*, *viii*, 37, 38, *39*
Sitwell, Edith 121
Shropshire hills 28, 104
Tailhade, Laurent 88, *89*

Tennyson, Alfred Lord 64, 81
Thomas, Edward 102
Uffington 15, 54, 56–59, *58*, 106
  Ferry *57*, 125
Uriconium Roman Site 61, 62, *63*, *64*, 70, 79, 122
Villa Lorenzo *86*, 87
War 4, 56, 59, 60, 65, 84, 85, 87, 88, 90, 91, 94, 98, 99, 101, 103, 105, 112, 113, 120, 122
  Outbreak 84, 94
  Relief 85
  Refugees 87, 90, 94
  Women's work 90, 91, *100*, 106
  German prisoners 92, 93
Wells, H.G. 109
Wigan, Revd Herbert 66, 68, 69, 73, 74, 123
Wordsworth, William 58, 64